T0247595

On Leadership

Also by Tony Blair

A Journey

TONY BLAIR

On Leadership

Lessons for the 21st Century

CROWN
NEW YORK

Published in the United States by Crown, an imprint of the Crown Publishing Group,
a division of Penguin Random House LLC, New York. First published in 2024 by
Hutchinson Heinemann, an imprint of Cornerstone. Cornerstone is part of
Penguin Random House group of companies.
crownpublishing.com

Library of Congress Cataloging-in-Publication Data has been applied for.

ISBN 978-0-593-79979-6
Ebook ISBN 978-0-593-79981-9

Printed in the United States of America on acid-free paper

Editor: Madhulika Sikka
Editorial assistant: Fariza Hawke
Production editor: Joyce Wong
Production manager: Heather Williamson
Publicist: Penny Simon
Marketer: Chantelle Walker

9 8 7 6 5 4 3 2 1

First American Edition

Jacket design by Ceara Elliot

*To the wonderful staff at my Institute
who are making change happen*

Contents

CONTENTS

CONTENTS

Leadership and the Science
of Governing

No Leader I ever met, who succeeded, did so just by being a "LEADER." They did it by hard work, by application, by poring over the detail, by agonising before deciding, by harnessing their self-doubt as well as their self-confidence.

And by curiosity. By a willingness to learn. By a relentless pursuit of the right answer, burrowing all the way down to the core, if necessary, to get it.

I was for ten years head of the British government and have spent almost twenty afterwards, through my institute, helping governments and Leaders in around forty different countries all over the world. I learnt a lot doing it and I have learnt a lot watching others do it.

Leadership is always a journey. Over time, I have deciphered a pattern in that journey broken into three stages.

In the first flush of taking power, Leaders are all ears. They know they know nothing or little of what governing truly means. They listen eagerly.

In the second stage, when they have become acclimatised to the rhythm of it all, they know enough to think they know everything. They're impatient with listening. They're the boss. Who can know more than them?

The third stage is that of maturity when they come to the realisation that what they know is not the sum total of political knowledge; that there are things—many of them—that they don't know. Once again, with more humility, they listen and learn.

That sweet arrival at discernment is unfortunately usually achieved by bitter experience.

The distance between the three stages can be long or short.

Many Leaders never get past stage two. And this is most often where the mistakes are made.

This book is about how, by studying the lessons and science of governing, Leaders can shorten the learning curve, steepen it and get to stage three faster and in better shape.

Governments have been around forever, of course. But the twentieth century saw an unprecedented expansion in what they do and in what the public expects of them.

In early-nineteenth-century Britain, the role of the state was very circumscribed. Governments raised taxes to pay for a limited set of duties that revolved mainly around defence. There was little or no public education system; no government-mandated healthcare system; no pensions and little welfare. The administration of law and order was rudimentary. The concept of social care was unknown. During the course of the nineteenth century state provision developed, but even in 1900, government expenditure accounted for only about 12 per cent of GDP.

Since then, as government has progressively taken on

more and more duties and responsibilities, that figure has risen to over 40 per cent. Most modern developed nations have built their public realm in much the same way. And developing nations are following suit.

People now rely on their government to organise—and often fund—the education of their children, to provide care when they're sick, and financial support when they're old or unemployed. They expect their government to keep the streets safe and the nation protected. They look to it to pass laws to administer an ever-more complex business environment, and to regulate everything from food production to waste management to the promotion of products to environmental and climate issues.

As a result, government today is a vast, sprawling, intrusive, all-encompassing behemoth in our lives. We may fiercely debate its size and purpose, but the reality is that it is here to stay, and at a level which makes how it functions a significant part of how our lives are led.

Yet, even though that truth is inescapable, the odd thing is how confined and rarefied is the debate about what we might call the science of governing: how the machine works and how it might be made to work better.

I don't mean we don't debate the competence or otherwise of particular governments or debate their policies. We do. But we don't focus much on the principles of what good governance looks like, what works and what doesn't, whether there are common rules or lessons we could learn. In other words, we don't pause to consider how to extract the best from this behemoth.

It is true that every country's circumstances are different.

And I find a very common belief among political Leaders, at least at the beginning of their mandate, is that their nation is *sui generis* and that there is a limit to what they can learn from others.

But the processes of government are firmly similar across nations. The challenges are often the same. The manner of governing—effective or ineffective—has the same characteristics. Governments also have decades of experience to draw on. It is therefore possible, and from the point of view of success essential, to be aware of—to understand—the various elements of government before taking on the burden of responsibility for the nation.

The way government functions, how it creates the right structures for decision-making, how it organises itself, how the leadership spends its time and uses its bandwidth for governing as opposed to politicking, is its own science.

Mastering this science is quite literally the difference between governments—and, therefore, often countries—that succeed and governments—and countries—that fail.

I do an exercise when talking to new Leaders whereby I invite them to consider countries which are next to each other and similar in terms of population, natural resources and opportunities, and then compare them.

Poland and Ukraine (before the war). Rwanda and Burundi. Myanmar and Malaysia. For all Colombia's problems, compare it with Venezuela. Or compare Kuwait with the most successful Gulf States. And then there's the greatest governing laboratory experiment available to humankind, the Korean peninsula—North and South Korea.

For each successful country, there will have been a

turning point, a moment when they moved ahead, developed, liberated potential and expanded.

How were the turning-point decisions formulated? How were they translated from vision to reality? Each step didn't just involve a thought but a way of proceeding: there was a policy, a framework for implementation, an executive process of delivery. Of course, there was also leadership.

So you would be unwise as a Leader to embark upon a major reform without closely studying how other Leaders facing similar problems and challenges have handled them. Governing offers lessons; it has attributes applicable as generalities. Even its idiosyncrasies have common elements. It repays study.

In a democracy we elect the head of government. There are, however, no other qualifications required for governing: I became prime minister without any prior experience of government. Leaders don't work their way up, learning as they go, with objective assessment of capacity; they just arrive and get on with it. The same is true of many, if not most, ministers, even though they run big departments and control large budgets. It's also true of countries which are not democratic: the new leadership takes office with the same discordance between power and experience; and their ministers are in the same boat.

In any other walk of life, most of which are of significantly less importance to the average citizen than government, no one would dream of such a thing. We would think it irresponsible, unwise and highly hazardous.

In fairness to the electorate, they can't really be expected to have a precise view of the fitness to govern of those they elect. They have a general opinion, of course, and in a democracy they choose on that basis.

But even though, when a new Leader comes to office, they may well be lacking in experience—their team likewise—they can compensate for the inherent irrationality of the system that got them there. There is a playbook they can examine; there are clear lessons which they can learn. Even if the journey is one which they have never made before, others have; there are route maps which can be followed, warning signs which can be read, and lived experience which can illuminate what governing really entails.

Such study can't compensate for the absence of leadership. But it is surely better if Leaders are educated by the available learning of how others have fared carrying the burden of leadership.

Every Leader will confront the challenges of devising strategy, policy, delivery, building the right team, overcoming the interests which stand in the way of reform, moving their bureaucracy from inertia to impact, of steering the domestic Ship of State through storms of external events.

So, whatever their natural qualities of leadership, there should be room for the taught qualities of leadership, for the tangible skills of design and implementation as well as the more ethereal element of character.

Politics is part philosophy, part performance and part practicality. The last is more mundane but it is the one which finally makes the difference.

For the person at the top, there is a difference between being a Leader and leadership. Or certainly a difference between being "A Leader" and merely the person occupying the position of leader.

Leaders arrive in positions of leadership by many varied routes: some by calculation, some by accident, some through circumstance, some through crisis and some through courage; often it is an amalgam of all these.

But only a few really deserve the title "Leader"; i.e., once there, they exercise what we call—as a compliment—leadership.

I have come to the conclusion that the attributes of leadership are the same whatever the leadership position—from running a country to managing a football team to heading a company or indeed any type of organisation, be it a shop or a community centre.

A Leader steps out when others step back. The mantle of responsibility is being passed around and the Leader willingly takes it upon their shoulders. OK, sometimes they drape it graciously around them and sometimes they snatch it before anyone else can get near! But in either case or somewhere in between, they're prepared to wear it.

But that merely gets you the position of Leader. Being "A Leader" means something different.

Leaders have the courage not to go with the flow. They speak up when others stay silent. They act when others hesitate. They take the risk, not because they fail to identify it as risk but because they believe a higher purpose means the risk should be taken.

They're prepared to say what needs to be said, including to their own supporters.

This is an essential part of political leadership, without

which little gets achieved. Any reasonably intelligent politician knows what their public wants to hear. So, saying it is
easy: playing to the crowd, loving their warmth, feeling their
praise, stirring them; watching as they follow each cadence,
every gesture, the rhythm of the speech building in intensity,
the waves of applause and approbation. Since time imme-
morial, politicians have made such speeches, delivered such
lines, and now they tweet such sharp 280-character remind-
ers of allegiance.

This performative politics has its place. Few Leaders will
survive without such moments. Creating them requires
talent. But it isn't the same as leadership.

Standing in front of a crowd that is expecting to be
pleased but instead being prepared to displease it. Spelling
out the truth rather than the shibboleth. Persuading, not
placating, the audience that is not naturally on your side.
Addressing the head and not the heart of those who are.

The willingness to take not just the mantle but what goes
with it should that mantle be worn seriously: the criticism
as well as the adulation, the necessity of decision and not
simply debate; of substance as well as shine; of advancing
and not just being; of action and not mere analysis; to resolve
the problem and not simply articulate it.

And to keep going even when it looks like defeat is as
plausible an outcome as victory; to retreat tactically, but
never strategically.

This is leadership.

And to realise that giving people what they want is not
the goal of leadership.

Surprising thought? Especially for a political Leader?

Surely doing what "the people" want is what politics is all about. No?

No. Now such a surprising thought needs careful clarification. Of course, the goal is to improve the lives of the people. To make them better off, happier, more able to fulfil their dreams and aspirations.

But that is not the same as giving them what they want at any one moment of time, of chasing down each surge of opinion and trying to meet it, of scanning the polls and acting accordingly, of agreeing to every demand rather than assessing its reasonableness, of measuring the validity of a point of view by the vehemence with which it is expressed.

The Leader sets out for the people what they need and not simply what they want. Otherwise, the Leader is just a follower.

I love the old line of Henry Ford, when asked about giving people what they wanted: "If I had asked people what they wanted, they would have said faster horses." In a similar vein, Steve Jobs said: "You can't just ask customers what they want and then try to give it to them; by the time you get it built, they'll want something new."

What applies in business applies also in politics.

To think of this as elitist is to misunderstand fundamentally the correct relationship between Leader and led. The Leader should do what he/she believes is in the interests of the people. If the people end up disliking the outcome, sack the Leader.

But the job of the Leader is to lead.

Some of what is described in the pages that follow is about the business of leadership—how to determine priorities, construct the right policy, build a good team; it's about how to handle the stress and strain of governing.

All these things make for a more successful time as Leader. And no amount of courage can overcome a debilitating limitation of competence.

But courage—doing what is right, not what is easy, being prepared to be unpopular as well as popular—is an almost inevitable accompaniment of successful Leaders.

This is for the very matter-of-fact reason that true Leaders are change-makers. And change is the hardest challenge of governing.

Change is resisted. Many have often tried and failed.

So stepping out to take on the challenge requires courage.

Think of any of the great Leaders, from the icons like Mandela to the country-transformers like Lee Kuan Yew, they all had to strike positions which brought opprobrium. Yet they persevered, frequently against the odds, not blindly but determinedly.

Any Leader who has ever attempted a great reform has known its price: the depletion of political capital; the opening up of opportunity to adversaries; the dislike, even hatred, of those opposed to the reform; the pressure on you, those around you, even your family, your friends; at times, the gnawing anxiety of whether it's really worth it.

Though you know before you start that there will be pain, it is still curiously surprising and deeply uncomfortable when the pain kicks in.

Dealing with all this is the obvious definition of political courage.

But many of the things I talk about in the following

pages, which might seem better defined as competence, also necessitate courage. Choosing the right team and keeping them loyal, for example.

All Leaders have an ego. But recognising your weaknesses and compensating for them, putting that ego in its box, relegating it behind leading effectively—that is a type of bravery.

Going outside your comfort zone, embracing new ideas, new people, new ways of looking at the world, all these make for better government, but they also reveal something about the character and the courage of the Leader.

Being honest with yourself when you have let others down, being able to say sorry and mean it, not holding a grudge, forgiving even when forgetting is hard or impossible, all these may help you survive as Leader, but they also necessitate the personal courage to be self-critical and self-aware.

One final reflection: this is not a book about my qualities or lack of them as a Leader. Rather, it is about what I have learnt.

What I achieved as a Leader is debatable and debated! But that is not the point of this book. What is offered here is not an example but a lesson. Naturally, my mistakes or achievements are part of the context for what follows. But they aren't the start or end point.

This book is about lessons in governance, about leadership, and how leaders can become "Leaders."

PART I

Taking Power

CHAPTER ONE

Be the Leader with the Plan

Every government, if it wants to be successful, if it wants to navigate the treacherous political landscape which will be its habitat, needs a plan. A route map. A destination.

And the Leader has to be in the driving seat.

George Kennan, the distinguished American diplomat who defined the USA policy of containment towards the Soviet Union in the 1940s and 50s, once remarked (paraphrasing Lewis Carroll and *Through the Looking-Glass*): "If you don't know where you're going, any road will take you there."

It's essential the Leader does know where they're going. They're driving the bus. Drive it with purpose and speed, the passengers will be sitting behind the driver giving unwanted or misplaced advice, with varying degrees of politeness—but nonetheless sitting in their seats. If for one moment the bus stops for the driver to ask directions and the passengers get off and start discussing it all, believe me they will never get back on that bus.

The word "government" is derived from the Greek *kubernao*, meaning to pilot a ship, as in Plato's phrase "the Ship of State." To steer a course, governments need a plan.

A "plan" is not the same as a collection of desirable objectives or highfalutin visions. Helmut Schmidt, Chancellor of

I

West Germany between 1974 and 1982, famously cautioned that politicians with "visions" should go and see a doctor.

A "plan" is a route map for governing. It sets out the destination, the milestones and, above all, the priorities. It forms the "why" and not simply the "what" or "how."

It focuses the mind of government; indeed in a certain sense it creates the mind of government.

The preparation that goes into drawing it up is intense. Bad plan: bad government.

It needn't and probably can't set out every detail. But it should describe accurately the essentials of what the Leader wants to achieve; it should act to mobilise the government, give direction to ministers, and be underwritten with a clear narrative.

It should allow the observer to know: what the Leader thinks about the state of the country; what is wrong; what should be put right; and the core principles of how the "putting right" will be done.

Fashioned correctly such a plan serves multiple purposes. Of course, it sets out a clear journey—we know where we're meant to be going at least. But, more than that, politically it defines the agenda. People can be for it or against it; but everyone is obliged to define themselves around it.

I always used to say that the thing that would make me feel most electorally vulnerable, was if I saw a governing plan coming down the track at me, which was better than the one I had.

Provided that the plan is properly worked out and is not just a wish list of aspirations, it becomes the pole of political debate. This calms the governing party and unnerves the opposition.

But working it out is more complex than it might appear. Crucially, it has to establish PRIORITIES: if you try to do everything you will likely end up doing nothing.

The plan should identify those things the Leader thinks are vital, that define success or failure for the project of governing, that show where energy will be principally directed, that reveal what the government is trying to keep and what it is determined to change.

Often these changes demand structural reform on a large scale. My experience of governing is that changes usually fit into two categories. First, there are changes which are one stroke of the legislative or administrative pen—such as abolition of a tax or setting a minimum wage. They're important. But the process of government in respect of them is relatively straightforward.

But then, second, there are the changes of a systemic nature—reform of healthcare, welfare, privatisation of a major state utility, for example—and these changes involve painstaking analysis of the system, the precise changes you want to make and their relationship to the system as it currently operates; they involve managing a range of different interests, all of which will fight the change or find ways to diminish or neuter it.

These changes are the tough ones; they will take time, they mean using up political capital, and you can't do too many. Hence, as I will describe, the need to prioritise.

The plan should at least give clarity of direction on these reforms, since beyond any doubt these are not just the hardest to do in practical terms, but the hardest for you to persuade the public that they need to be done.

They should begin as early as possible in the mandate because they take time.

And here democracy has set itself a challenge.

I reckon it takes ten years to change a country. And that is ten years of focused change-making. At a minimum. Fifteen is better and twenty optimum.

One president I work with came to power as the first person elected democratically in his country after a period of dictatorship; and to mark his determination not to fall into the bad ways of his predecessor, he committed to serving only two years of his term, after which he would hand on to someone else.

Very noble; but unfortunately, also very naive.

At our first meeting I told him bluntly that if he continued to govern on that basis: the system would not take his instructions seriously; his Cabinet would spend their time positioning for the succession, not working for the country; and he would not only be a lame duck but one that was effectively stationary.

Rather than the reputation of democracy being improved, it would be damaged because nothing would get done.

Fortunately, he decided to take my advice and, having been re-elected, is now beginning his second full term.

But even after two terms he will face a problem. If his successor is from a different party or dislikes his agenda, then the structural change he is attempting will lose momentum and stall.

Because the structural change will not be complete.

Such change takes time, and it takes a consistency of policy, and in a democracy, a degree of consistency through changes of government.

A good plan—well worked out with coherent policy-making underpinning it—not only gives the Leader the means of setting the agenda and governing effectively, it also gives the best chance of making the plan stick, because even though it will naturally be amended—bits will become redundant or irrelevant, not all of it will work as intended—the basic direction will be set with such force that it will take a better plan to derail it.

The plan should be drawn up with a rigorous attention to what is already in place. Whatever criticisms you have made of the previous administration—and let's assume there have been many, because that is in the nature of politics—judge impartially what is working and what is not. You don't have to reinvent everything. Just because "they" did it, doesn't mean it is wrong.

When I became prime minister in 1997, there were things from the period of my Conservative predecessors Margaret Thatcher and John Major I wanted to change; and things I felt were settled as a direction for the country and should remain.

So, we did not disturb the encouragement of private enterprise, much lower top rates of tax, privatisation of industries like telecoms that are better suited to market discipline, or the legal framework for industrial relations.

We also kept the core direction of foreign policy, at least around membership of the EU and a strong transatlantic alliance with the USA.

But we made big changes in the rebuilding of the public realm—health, education, law and order, welfare, children's services; we prioritised the poorest through tax credits and the minimum wage; and we changed radically the mood and policy around social and liberal issues such as gay rights.

So, there was a consistency of policy as well as significant change. That gave the business community particularly, at least up until the financial crisis and then Brexit, stability and predictability in policymaking.

But it arose as a result of, first, the Conservative government and then the New Labour government having a clear plan of what needed to be done, and why.

Of course, in one sense, any new government is a reaction to the last. But measure the consequences of that reaction assiduously.

Construct the plan with care; make it durable.

And design the strong centre which can deliver it.

CHAPTER TWO

Make the Centre Strong

Leaders often come to power with no executive experience. The skill set that makes for a good campaign to become Leader is not the same as the one required to be a good Leader, and indeed can be entirely inadequate once you're in office. You need to make a step change. The Great Persuader must, at a stroke, metamorphose into the Great CEO.

Campaigns are exhilarating things, carrying the aspirant along on a wave of hope and enthusiasm, and the risk is, if successful, the Leader believes in their own magic and treats governing as an extension of campaigning. This is a serious error.

Of course, when you're in power, communications, clear narrative and engagement with the people don't diminish in necessity. It is simply that the overriding challenge, once elected, is to govern and that means to deliver.

In opposition, it matters what you say. In government, it matters what you do. And saying is a lot easier than doing.

As was said earlier, governing is the one profession of importance in which a person with no qualifications, no track record, a CV devoid of content, can rise to a position of extraordinary power.

In any other walk of life, we would consider such a circumstance unthinkable, ridiculous even. A CEO who had never managed before; a maestro conducting the orchestra who had never held a baton; a pilot flying an aircraft with nothing more to guide them than a vague appreciation of aerodynamics—we laugh at the thought.

Imagine a Premiership football club, seeking a new coach, that said: hey, let's get the most enthusiastic fans together and do a hands up among them for who should get the job. The fans themselves would think that mad. And the team wouldn't last long in the Premiership.

But in politics this can happen.

Now, of course, a political Leader has knowledge of politics and, in a previous life, may have run an organisation outside of politics. But that is different from governing a country. Many magnitudes of difference.

When I entered 10 Downing Street in May 1997, I had never held any ministerial office. I started at the top, which in one way is excellent. But it took me time to adjust, and time to learn that government requires a completely different mindset and application from opposition.

You may have your plan. The direction should be clear. But you need to make sure that the immediate world around you is organised to deliver.

And this starts at the very beginning, or, to misquote Julie Andrews in *The Sound of Music,* at your own office.

Don't listen to those who tell you to have a light touch, to let your ministers "get on with the job," to assume that others in the chain of command will do what they're meant to do. The people who proffer this advice are either academics trained in theory not practice, or civil servants who know that a weak centre allows them to rest easy.

This is not the same as devolution of power within a state, where decision-making itself is better exercised at a local level and where there is a process for deciding leadership—for example, city mayors or local officials in a federal system or, in a country such as the UK made up of different nations, devolved institutions. I mean control of those areas for which you as head of government are responsible.

All bureaucracies are the same. They're not conspiracies for one side or another in politics; they're conspiracies for maintaining the system and they have a corresponding genius for inertia. They can be utilised and driven but should not be left with the first or final say, as I shall explain later.

Occasionally, a Leader will come to power and the country is in good shape (despite whatever criticisms that Leader may have levelled at their predecessor), and the task is good management, not change.

Fine. Then it is a little different. But I am addressing the Leader who wants to be a change-maker. And, in any case, rarely is the status quo satisfactory; otherwise, why would you be there?

The Leader needs a strong centre, a centre capable of initiating and carrying through change in an effective and timely manner.

The Leader has power precisely because they are the Leader. That is the position from which their authority is derived. Harness it wisely and things happen.

The strong centre is necessary because, without it, that authority is not able to be harnessed. It sits weakened or dormant. On the other hand, once the system knows that the centre is driving the agenda, it will respond: ministers will be put on notice, the purveyors of inertia become anxious and on the back foot.

But that strong centre won't happen of its own accord. Organising it is the Leader's first task.

It starts with something so obvious that many Leaders I come across miss it entirely: THE SCHEDULE!

When I was Leader of the Opposition in the UK and some time out from an election which we were expected to win, I visited President Clinton at the White House. As we began our set of meetings, he said: "Remind me to tell you something really important before you leave."

I was greatly taken with this and assumed I was about to have some huge secret of state imparted to me. As I was leaving, I reminded him. He looked at me very solemnly and said: "Whoever runs your schedule is the most important person in your world as Leader. You need time to think, time to study and time to get the things done you came to leadership to do. Lose control of the schedule and you will fail."

I confess I was a little underwhelmed at the time. But he was right.

Time is the most precious commodity. You can be absolutely sure that what appeared relatively straightforward when castigating the previous leadership of the country becomes a world more complex when you are faced with real life painted not in slogans but in complex prose. And without time to focus on delivery, to work out the right policies, to manage the politics of the changes you're making, you will find that the grand vision you elaborated on so confidently when in opposition will never translate into reality.

Chinggis (or Genghis) Khan—who, after all, did create one of history's most extraordinary empires—once said: "Conquering the world on horseback was easy; the hard part was when you had to dismount and govern."

And here is the challenge for the Leader. There are a million calls on your time. Foreign dignitaries stop by; necessary but ultimately—unless you're engaged in some mighty work which requires international engagement—a distraction.

Everyone wants something from you or wants to be with you. Fellow politicians, business folk, old and new friends. There are ceremonies to go to, funerals and weddings which can't be missed, occasions of state where the flummery is in inverse proportion to their impact on the lives of the citizens.

Many Leaders are in meetings from early morning to late night. Most of them unproductive. Every hour spent like this is an hour you cannot replace and diverts you from the real challenge of governing.

So, the person who runs the diary—that is, the schedule—and the people who have a say over what goes in it, have to be of the highest calibre and the closest connection to you. And they must operate under strict instructions.

You need to turn up to an event? Go, but spend no more than an hour there. Or less. The event organiser will complain, shout at your people, tell them that if you don't stay all night it will be deeply insulting and ruin your leadership. But your people must stand firm.

They should be smart enough, though, to judge. Sometimes you will have to stay all night. The point is: whoever is charged with the schedule has to have real skill, small "p" political sensitivity, charm when saying no.

As a Leader it's hard for you to say no; your inclination is always to say yes. That's why, behind you, you need the guard dogs who will hold firm even under the most intense pressure.

Your ministers want time with you. You have to see them, of course. But not whenever they wish.

Parliament takes time. When I changed Prime Minister's Questions from fifteen minutes twice a week in the afternoon to thirty minutes once a week at midday, I saved literally a day or a day and a half of prime ministerial time.

A Leader must keep in touch with their people. You go out into your country, seeing things first hand, meeting the locals, keeping up a constant patter of communications. All of this is important. But remember that a half-day trip is probably as efficient as a full day. Go in, meet, speak, leave.

You will have to see those foreign dignitaries. These relationships are important. But structure the visits. And minimise your own visits overseas. Again, they have to happen. But make the time spent effective, with as little protocol and as much proper substance as possible. Your people in charge of protocol are no doubt good people. They like their job. They like the fuss and fawning, the elaborate ceremony, the theatre of it all. But *you* shouldn't like it because, if you do, you will spend a lot of time doing it.

Time not focused on delivering what you're in government to do reduces your capacity to deliver.

I know Leaders who keep open house—and at first people love it: they bask in the Leader's light; it shows that they, too, are important. But quite quickly, and in government things always move far quicker than in opposition, the open house pales, the people demand action, their expectations become mired in disillusion, and without the time and space to focus, the government loses its shine and the Leader their light.

Then there is something that all too easily gets neglected: you also need time for yourself, for your family, for relaxing, for shedding the stress, if only for a moment.

Your schedule has to create that personal time. Throughout the day people are sucking the energy from you, and you are giving orders, making decisions, all of it tiring and draining. That personal time replenishes the mind and the spirit.

I know it seems odd to prioritise the schedule in the almost religiously observant way I am proposing. And I accept there are some Leaders who seem never to rest or lose concentration; but if you're an ordinary mortal, following these simple rules will pay a huge dividend in efficacy.

Then, naturally, there is the rest of the centre to organise.

The aim should be to create a machine competent to propel the Leader's agenda. I deal with the detail of this later, but, in essence, given that you need the centre to be strong, it needs to be organised for strength.

I reorganised the centre of government after winning my second general election, having learnt the lessons of governing from my first mandate.

In the first term, I beat the system over the head to make it move faster. And to a degree it did. But not enough, and when I stopped beating it, it slowed back down.

The reorganisation's purpose was to focus the centre, give it the capacity and capability it needed to drive the government, and hold it accountable—to me, but also to hold me accountable to my own intentions. And to be always on. Even when I was distracted.

My restructuring involved separate units dedicated to *policy*, *strategy*, *communications* and *delivery*.

The Delivery Unit concept is what that reorganisation is best known for and it is now widely replicated globally. Michael Barber was its midwife, did a brilliant job and wrote a book about it—*Deliverology*—which, I kid you not, sits on the bookshelves of many Leaders I know.

But the other innovations were equally important.

In the Policy Unit policy specialists can track the development of government policy and also suggest improvement or adjustment. It's important to note that these specialists should come not from government departments but from the Leader's own team, and should embody great analysis and policy capacity.

The Strategy Unit focuses on longer-term thinking which throws up new ideas and ways of looking at the world.

A Strategic Communications Unit is vital, of course, because otherwise a government seems technocratic rather than value- and mission-driven. It needs to provide communications of the strategic sort; i.e., not just for the next day's news but for consistency of explanation across government.

So, the centre of government must be strong enough to help devise policy, ensure strategic coherence, keep the plan on course, communicate it and, above all, deliver on it.

There will be crises, things which were never anticipated, events of a supervening nature, scandals, shocks and alarums and excursions, but throughout the Leader must have a machine relentlessly focused on achieving the objectives set.

Make the centre STRONG!

CHAPTER THREE

Prioritisation: Try to Do Everything and You Will Likely Do Nothing

I often say to new Leaders that a good way to approach governing is through what I call the four P's: prioritisation, policy, personnel and performance management.

The first—prioritisation—is much harder than it seems.

You come into government with a manifesto. It is usually detailed. It has to touch all the electoral bases. It is supposed to be a plan for government. But the reality is it isn't. That's not its purpose. Its purpose is to be part of a (winning) campaign. Even if drafted with care and discipline, it is a list of the desirable, not necessarily the doable, and it is written with the uplifting rhetoric of hope rather than the more dour honesty which a true plan for government entails.

There's a joke I was once told by a Catholic priest about religion which could be applied to politics as well. A group of the deceased arrive at the pearly gates to be met not as they anticipated by St. Peter but by the Devil, who says to them: "Look, before you meet St. Peter, let me first show you the choices, because I get an undeserved bad reputation and it's important you know them." They say OK and he shows them heaven, where the people are peacefully relaxing, talking in quiet undertones respectfully, reading the odd improving book and generally behaving. Then he shows them hell: there are wild parties, drinking and debauchery, everyone indulging with abandon and abundance.

Wow, they think, we never knew hell was like that. They go back up to the pearly gates and say to St. Peter: "It's really nice of you to offer us heaven but, um, no offence, we really would prefer to go to hell." So, off they go. They enter hell and there is wailing, gnashing of teeth, it's cold, miserable and horrible. They see the Devil standing there surveying it all and angrily accost him, saying: "Hey, what's happening? Where are the parties and drinking and debauchery, the living it up, and all those great things you promised?"

"Ah, well," says the Devil, "back then I was campaigning."

The campaign and its manifesto are the guide to winning, but they're an unsuitable guide to governing, except in describing what you hope will happen, and they rarely prioritise with the rigour that, once you assume power, is absolutely vital.

As I said, if you try to do everything, you will likely end up doing nothing.

When I first entered Downing Street as a new prime minister, I was met by the Cabinet Secretary, at that time a grand and significant figure in the UK system for sure, who told me proudly that the Civil Service had been reading the manifesto and drawing up plans for implementation. He meant well, naturally. After eighteen years of Conservative government, he wanted to show that the system accepted the legitimacy of the new masters.

But I confess I was somewhat alarmed at the notion that what they might think were the priorities would not coincide with what I thought were the priorities; and I had to explain that the manifesto was a document of intention, not a defined plan for government.

Government operates by bandwidth. One of the challenges arising out of Britain's decision to leave the European Union—and let us tactfully, for these purposes, leave aside the rights and wrongs of the decision—was that it took up a huge amount of the bandwidth of governing. It extracted an immense part of the political energy from the system, shortening the concentration span available for other things.

There is no shame in being frank about this. No minister—including and perhaps especially the prime minister—and therefore no government can focus on all problems in the same way. There isn't the time and there isn't the mental capacity.

So, a government in its ministries will get on with a range of different things and try to cover the entire landscape and that's as it should be. Some things matter more than others, though, either because they are important objectively or because, subjectively, they're priorities for the government or the minister. You need a process for determining what they truly are and be clear there can't be too many of them.

Now, of course, in one sense everything is a priority. When I made my first party conference speech as Leader I expressed the first three priorities of an incoming government as: "education, education and education." Great line. Made the necessary impact. But I remember next day meeting someone who said to me: "So healthcare doesn't matter any more?"

You can't as a Leader ever say that something isn't a priority. You're addressing the arts community and are asked: "Is culture a priority?" Or you're making a speech to the development community and you're posed the same question about aid as a priority. What are you going to say? "Nah, not really"?

Which, for the avoidance of doubt, is not to say that either is unimportant. Both are very important. But they won't determine whether you're in government or not.

But there are things which define the government and you as Leader.

A good way to identify them is to imagine you're making a speech for your re-election. What is it ideally that you would want to be able to say you have achieved? You're never going to convince people you have done everything; but what is it that defines you as having at least done something?!

Work back from that and you will have the answer to your priorities. You might not really have understood them until you work out what it is you want to say you have done.

Of course, "something" must have been done, and to have been done, it had to have been doable.

And doable means not only worthy of being done but practically achievable.

I once advised a Leader who was discussing with me his

top priority, which was a massive infrastructure project. There was no doubt that it would have been transformative. It was a big, bold and beautiful idea. "It's a game-changer," he said to me confidently. "But what makes you think it can be done and financed?" I asked. To which he had no convincing answer. I advised him to check out its feasibility before he made a political commitment that pinned his fortunes to a mast whose robustness he had not adequately investigated.

You can have a goal and fail. But you should at least know it has a serviceable chance of success before spending energy and political capital on it.

The priorities are the big things, and because they're big, there can't be fifteen of them. If you're lucky you will make five. And the process of prioritisation must begin at the beginning of the government. Otherwise, effort is diffused, or events drive the agenda.

The system—by which I mean the government departments, the Civil Service and the associated public sector agencies—needs direction at the outset. That does not guarantee the system will agree on each priority's importance, but it will know for sure what you consider important.

This is crucial because each minister and each ministry will have their own pet projects or their own ideas as to what really matters.

You are the CEO of the organisation. You have a certain amount of political capital. Any good change usually requires the expenditure of some of that capital. If you don't carefully spell out the priorities, you will find the capital is being spent on things your senior team may care deeply about, but that you don't believe are worth your capital they're depleting.

This process of prioritisation, therefore, is not just about the obvious fact you can't do everything, it is also a political framework which shapes your government.

So, don't take this process casually, or let it come about of its own accord. Focus on it, treat it as an essential part of the road map, not only for the first term but an essential component of the route-finder for getting another.

Once you have your set of priorities fixed, you need the policies to implement them.

CHAPTER FOUR

Good Policy Is (Nearly) Always Good Politics

I used to say to my children: "Work hard, play hard = possibility of success; play hard, work hard = virtual certainty of failure." The order is important. There are always those who defy the odds. But I can say that, almost without exception, anyone at the top of any profession, from business to sport, that I have met followed the "work hard, play hard" order. (Or only worked hard, of course!) In the music business, I did know folk who succeeded while apparently focusing on playing extremely hard. But in the end, they either corrected themselves or their career declined.

The same rule applies to politicians. For government the equivalent reads: policy first, politics second. In other words, decide the right policy to solve the problem and then fashion the right politics around it; don't decide the politics and then form a policy to suit.

In general terms, and contrary to much received political wisdom, the best politics usually derives from the best policy. This is not universally true and may at any given moment seem apparently untrue. But on the whole, good policy has a good outcome, bad policy a bad one; and the Leader has to believe that, over time, people notice.

A myriad of things gets in the way of good policy. Short-term politics frequently militates against it. Interests vested in the status quo fear and fight it. Distractions put the government off course. And occasionally a changing reality renders a once good policy bad.

However, just as the public like a government with a plan, because they feel it knows what it wants and therefore to a degree what it is doing, and so gives them confidence, they will listen to a government which sets out a policy with belief. They will listen most closely if that conviction seems clearly derived from sound analysis.

During the Covid-19 crisis in the UK, for example, there was some understandable anxiety about the programme of mass vaccination, with vaccines being developed at unprecedented speed, and with the normal timelines for research and trials suspended. There was resentment at restrictions on our daily lives, at having to wear masks, take innumerable tests and all the wretched panoply of Covid measures we had never experienced before.

In retrospect, no doubt mistakes were made and aspects of policy, or the application of policy, wrong.

And there are those who still today rail against the whole business and think those of us who advocated it are quasi-fascist.

But they're a minority. Most people accepted vaccination was necessary (and FYI the roll-out of the vaccine in the UK decisively cut serious illnesses and deaths).

And most accepted there had to be at least some restrictions.

This was because the policy appeared to be rooted in a

genuine and sensible policymaking process. The emergency meant that though everything was happening at speed, it also had huge focus from government, constant running explanation and experts in support.

And so, again in the end, the politicians who took the evidence-based approach, who stood out against populist ranting about vaccines and restrictions, managed to come through relatively politically unscathed. I can't think of a single Leader in a Western democracy who lost power by having a strong commitment to a worked-out Covid policy.

The policy was well developed partly because of the enormous effort and time devoted to it in government. For two years, it was the only priority. The country was battling something extraordinarily serious and affecting everyone directly in one way or another.

So, this is a great example of policymaking but also in unique circumstances.

Much harder is to take that framework of policymaking and transfer it across wide swathes of policy applied to normal times.

And to avoid it being driven by what is politically convenient rather than what is intellectually correct. Policy born of ideology or convenience distorts analysis, preconceives in bias that which should be conceived through evidence, and reinforces rigidity in a world constantly changing and therefore requiring openness to new thinking.

I often used to say in Cabinet, or in discussion with close advisers, first let's try to work out the right answer. We can get to the politics later. But what is the right analysis of the problem we're trying to solve? What are the facts? What might be a solution which really works?

And don't think about the issue as a politician. If we're debating education, think about it as a parent. If the topic is healthcare, think about it like a patient. If crime, like a victim.

The best policy starts with those questions from that perspective and then the politics is layered on top once the answer is decided.

At one level politics is a crude retail business: winning votes, devising slogans, kissing babies and having the physical stamina to survive a brutal campaign. But at another level—the dimension called government—it is an intensely intellectual exercise. It requires real brainpower. And study.

Politicians become adept over time at speaking about things they haven't a clue about. And, if they're good at it, they can do it with panache and—to the uninformed ear—credibility.

In the real world of government that doesn't cut it. You should know what you're talking about because you have taken the time and effort to master it.

Governments should also work with people who are actually doing what a government is proposing to affect by laws or administrative decision. I always found that interaction with the people in the front line of public services gave insights that no amount of briefing papers could uncover. Deep consultation with the business community would save a lot of errors if it was conducted in a spirit not of suspicion but partnership.

Ensure that policymaking is a collaborative effort, not in

the sense that you opt for consensus and the lowest common denominator, but in the sense of reaching out to those who may have an interest and also the imagination to think beyond it, or to those who are actively seeking change in the area they work in and know about.

Treat policymaking not as a spasmodic response to the difficulty of the day but as an opportunity to go deep and make change which lasts: a change not a splash.

And though the Leader should not get lost in detail, they must know enough, and therefore understand enough, to be satisfied that the policy meets the objective.

In this exercise, be careful not to arrive at an approach by halves. By this I mean sometimes you have worked out with your team what the right answer is, but then have to take account of political realities that may be so strong they threaten to overpower the policy. But gauge the strength with caution. If you have to compromise, OK. But within the margin between "have to" and "choose to" lies a critical test of leadership. Every step away from where on the right analysis you need to be is a defeat of sorts. So don't willingly surrender to it out of a desire for an easier life. Do so only if forced by necessity.

Take immigration, an issue bedevilling the politics of every Western country. Our economies depend on it. But it also imposes a cultural strain. My view has always been that provided there are rules, we will avoid prejudices. It is an issue of order. Most people can accept that a certain level and type of immigration is economically essential, but they worry when they think the whole system is broken.

This is sometimes seen as a numbers game and it can be

so, if the numbers immigrating are very large. But, primarily, it's about control, about ensuring the means to decide who has a right to come to your country, rather than allowing immigration to be the consequence of the immigrant's own determination to come because the system itself is failing. And effective enforcement is critical.

The reality, therefore, is that if you want consent for the immigration the economy needs, then you must reflect in your policy what society demands. Hence the argument for digital ID: if you have that in place, with the necessary safeguards, the government knows exactly who has a right to be in the country and who doesn't.

I appreciate all the arguments about privacy and the fears expressed about government having people's data. But the world is moving towards digital ID, in any event, as a means of helping the citizen interact with government more directly and effectively; and it is a short step from there to using it as a control mechanism for migration. The alternative is a sense there are no controls which then feeds anti-immigrant sentiment in a way that is both economically and socially detrimental.

In other words, the right answer has to take account of political reality; it just shouldn't be abandoned because of it.

Recognise what you can learn from others. Comb the world for the best ideas. Leaders often think their country's problems are unique. This leads to the invariably incorrect assessment that the solutions likewise will be unique.

A Leader can learn so much from other countries' expertise. All over the globe countries are grappling with similar challenges: how to reform or—in much of the developing world—how to initiate systems of education and healthcare; how to digitise government and the economy. Among poorer nations, where agriculture remains the main source of employment, there are many with large areas of highly fertile land who nevertheless struggle to produce enough and get that produce to market, and who therefore find themselves forced regularly to import basic foodstuffs.

Every country I know is working out how to modernise their infrastructure and how to make the most of public–private partnerships. You can pretty much guarantee that someone somewhere is trying to do what you're trying to do. Some are succeeding. Copy them; or at least learn from their experience.

Bring in the best brains from wherever in the world they may be. Policy nationalism—"we know best how to solve our problems and don't need outsiders telling us what to do"—is crass. It simply means that the country is governed by the constraints of its systems and home-grown talent rather than enlarging capability beyond them.

Singapore affords a good lesson here—as in so many things. Under its first prime minister, Lee Kuan Yew, Singapore unashamedly imported the business and human capital it needed to flourish. Today it exports both. But without the first, it could never have done the second. A more unusual example would be the flourishing Korean arts community. First came decades of study of Western film and music. And there then followed this extraordinary Korean version of both which has taken the arts world by storm.

Finally, policymaking has a more immediate and then a

longer-term dimension to it. Especially in a world brimming with new thinking, it is hard to keep up with the evolution of ideas around policy. In Downing Street, we therefore had a Strategy Unit operating alongside the Policy Unit. The purpose of the former was to ensure the latter was working in alignment with the trend of intellectual thought.

The Strategy Unit contained a cadre of top-quality people, usually from outside the system and usually on secondment as a break from their conventional careers. Their task was to map out where the future might go, so that present and future policy had a relationship to each other. Today, more than ever, this function within government is vital.

Various international examples illustrate the point.

Singapore determined some years back to become the pharma hub of Asia (just as the UK could lead the world in life science if it used the NHS data it possesses as a platform).

The manufacturing giants of South Korea (a country which in the 1960s had the same GDP per head as Sierra Leone) or Taiwan didn't arrive by accident but by careful partnership between government and private sector.

Silicon Valley itself originated from research and science to improve the US military and defence capability. And think of the contribution Bell Labs made to the American economy and to technology.

The United Arab Emirates is one of the foremost countries today in the field of artificial intelligence. It started on that journey a decade ago. But it thought ahead strategically.

None of these groundbreaking initiatives would have happened without government having the capacity and the leadership to think ahead.

But the quality of the thinking is only as good as the quality of the thinkers.

CHAPTER FIVE

It's All About the People

There are some things so obvious in life that to state them seems otiose; and yet, though obvious, you can point to countless examples in your own career—I certainly can—of where the obvious has been ignored.

Foremost among these is the basic truth: it's all about the people. By this I mean not "the people" but the personnel the Leader chooses to surround themselves with.

In any field of endeavour, in whatever situation requiring leadership, this is essential. In politics it is mission critical. Wherever my institute works in the world, and I sit with and observe Leaders, I can tell which ones have teams that function well and which ones don't. And I can almost guarantee that those Leaders with poorly functioning teams will fail.

One of the most important first challenges of leadership, therefore, is to pick the team under you. These are the people who will execute your design, interface with stakeholders, guide you, sustain you in the tough times, be your eyes, ears and, at points, brain.

There don't need to be that many of them. I used to say: give me three or four smart people and we can transform a department. I was lucky in Downing Street that I had a truly outstanding group of people helping me.

Those in the immediate circle of the Leader need to be

clever—clearly; hard-working—of course; but they also need to possess other qualities, especially in politics. They need to be tough and, in situations of stress, able to cope, confident enough to fight back, willing to bend but only when necessity demands.

They should be unafraid to tell you the truth or to disagree. In many systems, because of the culture of a country, the Leader's team will be deferential to the point of sycophancy. But Leaders need to be challenged. Internal debate is healthy not disruptive. And there should be the trust between the Leader and their team that allows such debate. Once a decision is made, then, obviously, everyone needs to get behind it. But the quality of the decision will be greatly affected by the quality of the debate which preceded it. Respect for the Leader is crucial. Adulation is misguided.

At the same time, the team needs to be sensitive to the enormous pressure leadership puts upon political Leaders. Even today, having been a prime minister for ten years, I sometimes forget how easy it is to criticise and how hard it is to do. Leaders need their confidence boosting, even as they're being told uncomfortable truths. The team, in celebrating good news, should never keep the bad hidden. But, in the peculiar circumstances of politics, there is a fine line between frankness and destroying self-belief, and the team has to be able to tread that line with subtlety.

The team should be loyal to the Leader. They must also be loyal to each other. Throwing colleagues under the bus when the going gets rough is one of the least admirable characteristics I know. Yet it's common.

Really good people are hard to come by. In any walk of life exceptional talent is, well, exceptional. So, if you see someone with such talent, then go after them; if they're as good as you think they are, you will never regret it.

And never be afraid of having around you people smarter than you are. Avoiding doing so is a chronic leadership failing. Doing so will ultimately only make you look better!

That said, no one is irreplaceable. People, no matter how good, can burn out in a profession as raw and brutal as politics. I made the mistake several times of wanting to keep people who knew their time was up when I didn't. Your team should be a support not a prop. Habit can't stand in the way of efficiency.

If you're the Leader of a country, one big advantage you possess is that you have huge pulling power. You ask someone to come and work with you and, most times, the answer is yes. It may take some persuasion, some pursuit of the target, but in the end most people are patriotic and if their president or prime minister needs them, they will respond affirmatively to the call. That's why searching for the right people is rarely wasted time. The pursuit is worth it.

Crucial is a policy team that is smart, capable, without its own agenda and obedient to yours.

It will nearly always involve the input of outside experts. Political Leaders should not be captivated by experts, but should be respectful of them. They should not decide policy, but they should at least inform it.

However, I notice two features of today's world relevant to policy: the world is moving so fast that a Leader struggles to keep up with the new; and because of the complexity associated with systemic change, you need specialists to guide you.

As our knowledge expands, particularly in science and technology, so the generalist is giving way to the specialist. In fact, you can see this trend replicated in virtually every walk of life—in specific fields of medicine, in the law, from the provision of services to engineering.

This poses an additional problem for most civil services today. The civil servant, no matter how bright, has no realistic chance whatever of competing in knowledge and expertise with someone who is devoting their lives to a study or practice of a specialist subject.

So it's sensible for governments in this environment to pull in people from the outside, to open up to temporary secondments from other domains, private or public, and enlarge the space for innovative or at least intelligent and well-informed policymaking. Unfortunately, misguided anxieties about conflicts of interest, and unease at allowing strangers into the inner sanctum, often deter such openness. Such feelings should be resisted.

The "team," however, also includes ministers, and this is a whole different bouillabaisse.

I always divide ministers into two categories: those you want to choose and those you are obliged to choose. The former are the people you pick with enthusiasm; the latter are picked for you by politics. Every Leader will know that there are those you have to keep on your side for various political reasons—balance of factions, debts of honour or loyalty, skills which may not be entirely suited to managing a department, but which nonetheless are very useful in managing the government.

The important thing here is to put the people you want because of their ability in the most important jobs, and those appointed out of political necessity in positions where they have status but little practical impact. In other words, the roles which determine whether the government will deliver or not must be given to the people who can help carry the burden towards political success.

Let's say education is a top priority and you know it requires major reform. Put the wrong minister in charge and you will never get the programme delivered in the way you want. The reforms either won't happen or will happen ineffectively. The focus won't be there and, in the absence of strong political direction, the system will take over and the energy to reform will be absorbed and dissipated. The job has to go to the minister with the talent to see things through.

Not only should you make sure that the best ministers are in the key roles, you should also be unafraid to promote those who exhibit particular talent. That may seem an odd thing to say. Surely you reward talent with greater responsibility and influence? In politics, however, it is often the case that Leaders feel threatened by talented ministers, and fear that promoting them will create potential challengers for the top job.

This is a mistake. Failure to promote talent plainly and adversely affects the efficiency of the government. Less plain is that it is also pointless. True talent will find its own way. There's a risk, too, that the resentment caused by keeping the talent down, for fear of a challenge, will increase the likelihood of a challenge being mounted.

No Leader can make the changes a country's future demands by themselves. They need a team. That team must be the best on offer. Second-rate teams make for second-rate achievement and insubstantial change.

Part of the job of the team is to work with the bureaucracy. And in optimal circumstances, some of the high-performing bureaucrats will become an integral part of the team.

CHAPTER SIX

Curb Your Bureaucracy
but Cultivate It

All Leaders have to deal with their bureaucracy. The dreaded "system"! Every country has one. It comes in varying degrees of size, competence and effectiveness. At some point, and for some Leaders quite soon after starting, that system will become frustrating/confusing/enraging.

It is thus very important to know what bureaucracies are and what they aren't; what is reasonable to expect of them and what isn't.

Nearly all of them have some common characteristics. They regard themselves as permanent and the Leader as temporary. OK, if you're a long-standing dictator it may be different—though the system can still think an act of man or God can change that.

They know from experience that risk is rarely rewarded, and caution even more rarely punished. So, their default setting is to advise against action of a transformative nature, and to create a mood of hesitation in the mind of the Leader.

The civil servants are usually generalists. They have broad experience which can be immensely useful; but they lack specialist knowledge. This can be hugely limiting and means it is unwise to trust them with issues that require expertise.

Above all, they deal in process. Process is their game. Before anyone is sniffy about process, it does matter. It is a worthy means to an end. The trouble is its tendency to become the end, to take on a life of its own, thereby extinguishing creativity and innovation and embroiling the desired objective of policy in a continuous loop of deliberation not decision.

Therefore, the Leader has to curb the bureaucracy's natural inclination to be, well, bureaucratic—hence the importance of obtaining outside advice, for leadership grip, for ensuring the "system" is directed and not merely engaged.

Concentrate, too, on making the process genius of the bureaucracy as efficient as possible. Precisely because it matters.

I know of governments whose Cabinet meetings are endless. I can think of long, impenetrable briefings that consume whole forests of paper, where if there is a decision to be made it is lost somewhere in the middle of it all, unseeable by the normal eye. I have seen ministers—already daunted by their own subject area—expected to master a host of others with no guidance and little appetite. Just a vast mass of quite unstructured facts and analyses that sits on the decision-making like a huge meal you feel will never be digested.

So it is worth paying attention to the processes right at the start of getting the reins of power in your hands. Don't assume anything about the system. Not what it can do or what it can't. Treat it like a job applicant. Assess its cap-abilities and its friendliness or willingness.

The top civil servant is a very important appointment. And yet it's surprising how many new Leaders take over government and simply accept without question or investi-gation who is leading the machine supposedly under their command.

Realise there is no great mystique about the bureaucracy. It is part of the public sector much like any other part. That is to say its cadres are a mix of the genuinely public-spirited, the very able, the less able and the jobsworth. Its benefit is that it is a public service. Its disbenefit is that it is not subject to the skill-honing, talent-seeking discipline of the market. Or not to the same degree.

You should curb its bureaucratic impulse; but you can cultivate its public-spirited one. The issues a bureaucracy deals with are not lacking in importance. They affect real people's lives. And there are, within any system, those who recognise this, have a sense of duty about it and will work hard to fulfil that duty.

Naturally, too, there is also ambition. For those with ambition it is vital that they understand from the Leader what is likely to crown that ambition with promotion. Put the emphasis on results, on delivery, on getting things done, and those with ambition will respond. Reward improve-ments in process that aid improvements in substance and, very soon, the message will percolate down.

Energise it with clarity of direction and purpose and the system will adjust and reorient—and will do so quite happily.

Chaos, absence of grip, these are the things which awaken bureaucracy's inner inertia. Rather like some animals when they sense danger, the bureaucracy goes into self-protect mode, gathering in its exposed parts and lying still, waiting for the environment around it to settle and be commanded.

Government departments are notorious for becoming silos, i.e., self-contained places where only one idea is stored, places which encase that idea from being infected by others. The problem is that life doesn't fit with siloed ideas. Most government challenges require different departments to work in cooperation with each other and with the outside world. The Leader needs to create the spaces for such cooperation where the silos are opened.

One of the reasons why the centre of government has to be strong around the Leader is so that there is an overview of the programme that makes sure the parts fit together, that one part of government is not operating in contradiction, defiance or ignorance of another which could have a bearing on the programme's objectives.

Can the bureaucracy be trained or reskilled? Most Leaders with experience of governing are sceptical. But the true answer is: to an extent. And as with everything else, the pervasive impact of technology means that some training and reskilling is essential.

I can't think of a Leader who has come to the end of their leadership without quite strong opinions of their "system." Those opinions vary. But what they have in common is a feeling that even after a longish spell in government, the one never fully understands the other. For the Leader the system is rather like a picture you like but are never quite sure where to hang it in the house.

I guess this is because the Leader feels, at first, that, to switch simile, the bureaucracy is like an instrument in their hands. It may be ungainly and unwieldy or it may be sleek and smart. But it's possible to learn how to use it.

However, in time, the Leader appreciates that it isn't an instrument; it is a living organism. It has a mind and a temperament. So, while it can still be used and craves use by a good Leader, it can't be owned or bent completely to the Leader's will.

Bureaucracy is good for some things; bad for others. It will try to carry out orders but not past its own estimation of its capacity. If it obstructs, it can do so with a guile fatal to a Leader's programme. If it assists, it can be an effective helper, but it will never be a substitute for the Leader and their team.

So, as I say, worth paying attention to!

PART II

Delivery

CHAPTER SEVEN

Democracy or Not, It's All About Delivery

Whether a Leader is operating in a Western-style democracy, a "managed" form of democracy, a benevolent autocracy or is a "strongman" Leader, it is always about delivery.

I believe democracy is the best and highest form of government. But I also believe that it has become used to assuming its superiority; and we now live in an era where it must prove it.

A couple of decades ago when I would visit a country that was not a democracy, the Leader would half apologetically explain that his country was not yet ready for a democratic experiment, but in time, it was implied, it would get there. There was an acceptance that democracy is what a country should aspire to.

Now it is different. Those Leaders of non-democratic countries who are reasonable and open-minded people don't despise democracy as a dictator might; but they question it, question its stability, its media environment and, above all, its ability to take decisions and implement them. In other words, on the central challenge of governance—"getting things done"—they are unconvinced.

I point out that of the countries with the highest living standards today, the overwhelming majority are democracies, that the world's most powerful country—the USA—is a democracy and that, by and large, more people want to move to such countries than leave them—always a good sign.

It is a powerful argument historically. And it remains clearly powerful when we see how the freedom inherent in democracies allows innovation to flourish and private enterprise to feel unthreatened by state corruption or confiscation. The rule of law, as we shall see, is a huge advantage which most democracies have and by and large non-democracies lack.

But when it comes to governance, the riposte I hear too often is: you—meaning Leaders of democratic nations—have lost the capacity for long-term thinking or planning, your policymaking takes second place to your politicking, and your media environment means you're constantly managing crises which are of marginal importance to the future of your nations, while at the same time not focusing on the big things which will determine it.

In other words, an argument that we might have thought of as conclusive no longer seems so. Moreover, scepticism about democracy is no longer confined to more authoritarian regimes: it's also expressed by many citizens of democratic countries.

Now, for other elements of Western society, particularly parts of our media, the reason for democracy's failings is clear. For them, it's all about "transparency" or "accountability." Are governments "honest"? Are politicians "trustworthy"?

For parts of the international development and aid community, it's all about human rights.

These are somewhat different ways of saying that democracy is morally challenged and that its cure lies in "exposing" enough wrongdoing, having Leaders who "tell the truth," and putting it all out in the open, so to speak. If we do that, the argument goes, we will get great Leaders who will, in close alliance with "the people," make our lives better.

For the avoidance of doubt, I am not saying these moral questions aren't important or are immaterial to governing— at a certain level of development, they're crucial. But not at any stage of development should they outweigh delivery.

The challenge of democracy today is efficacy. Even if a democracy has a wonderful record on transparency, it won't trump a lousy record on delivery.

And in a developing nation, where people struggle to put food on the table, go to school, get rudimentary healthcare, eke out an existence not a career, delivery can be the difference between life and death; or at least the difference between a life with hope and one without it.

Of course, people want "honest" politicians, Leaders they trust; but above all what they want are solutions. They want the problems impacting their lives solved or at least mitigated. They want a higher standard of living, a better quality of life, improved healthcare and education, security.

These can't be simply the product of good intentions honestly expressed; they come from the implementation of policies which work.

Let us dig deeper. Take a classic Western democracy. The

reality in too many countries is that—contrary to the rule I set out earlier—politics comes first and policy second. The short term eclipses the long term. The political class seems often happier discussing a scandal than a solution.

Social media, in addition, creates a toxic environment for debate and a climate of genuine hatred and therefore risk for elected representatives.

Instability is as pronounced a feature of Western democracy today as stability. Traditional parties are being blown up by varieties of populists; splinter parties come and go. The politics of grievance predominates among significant parts of the electorate. All over Europe parties which used to hold power for long periods of time are crumbling. In the USA both traditional parties are uneasy coalitions of discord. In just eight years, between 2016 and 2024, the UK had six prime ministers. When I left office, I was the third in almost thirty. No wonder the country has a problem. How could it not?

The root cause of the instability is a failure to deliver. Since the financial crisis, living standards for many have stalled. Anxiety over immigration rages but no one seems to be able to solve it. Public spending is high; taxes commensurately high; outcomes in public services are low. Welfare spending doesn't appear to be effective in meeting societal pressures. Crime, especially organised crime, and disrespect for national institutions, of pride for the majority, seem to go unchecked. Conventional politicians proclaim they have solutions, but experience has taught people to doubt such protestations.

This is why populism is on the march. It really isn't

complicated. If conventional democratic politics doesn't seem to work, the person promising the biggest shake-up, creating the most stir, provoking the most outrage among the conventional, succeeds.

Everything in this book is designed to explain why delivery, making the change which works, is the only real test of government. But it is also the only way to protect democracy.

In the developing world, the context is different. But the lesson is the same. Here honesty and transparency can more vitally affect systems which impact efficacy. Corruption is the bane of delivery. Not only because it is morally wrong, but because it is a bad guide to decision-making. It spoils the opportunity for improvement in institutions and creates precisely the wrong spirit for enterprise and innovation to flourish.

But outside of this issue, any country today can make progress if it follows the principles of good governance. And by this, I mean not just "honest" governance but, above all, effective governance—in other words, they put systems and policies in place which can deliver. What is the best way of entrenching democracy in a country with only a nascent tradition of democratic government? Show it works!

If Western governments put as much effort into development policies that helped developing countries deliver practical solutions as they do in giving lectures on constitutional propriety, they and those they genuinely seek to help would be better off.

OK. Having made the case for efficacy as the most important ambition for government, and pointing out why Western democracy often has failings which managed democracy and benevolent autocracy often don't, let me state the corrective.

"Managed" democracy and "benevolent" autocracy only work if the managers remain smart and the autocrats remain benevolent. They fail if, for whatever reason, they morph into the "strongman" category.

As with everything else, there are no doubt exceptions, but "strongman" government, most times, doesn't work.

Such governments have one very big drawback, which isn't only to do with the principle of the thing, but goes to the heart of efficacy and delivery. Where there are no checks and balances on the exercise of power, because everyone is too terrified to disagree, bad decisions result.

Two recent examples stand out from countries which have led the charge against liberal democracy: Russia and China.

If Russia were a proper functioning democracy, the president of the country would never have made the extraordinary miscalculation that Ukraine—for all its flaws a true democracy with an elected president—would lie down and—given the history between the countries—let its neighbour walk all over it. No two genuine democracies have ever gone to war and for good reason. Their people prefer to live in peace and sort out disputes without military conflict. Whatever the outcome, the devastating consequences of this miscalculation for Russia—as well as, obviously, Ukraine—will last a generation. It came about because the Russian leader created an infrastructure around him denuded of the capacity to challenge.

China received praise for its initial handling of

the Covid-19 pandemic. Its death rates were vastly lower than those in Western countries. It pursued a policy of zero Covid-19 and for a time that policy seemed to have worked. In the USA and Europe, by contrast, partly by political choice and partly because of popular hostility shown towards lockdowns, the disease was initially left to run through the population, before lockdowns stabilised the situation and the virus was then brought under control through the building up of significant levels of natural immunity and by mass vaccination.

The advent of the Omicron variant, which was massively more contagious, changed the game and should have changed the policy of China. But because the leadership had pinned its colours to the mast of zero Covid, it couldn't or wouldn't adjust. The very omnipotence of the leadership created rigidity, not flexibility. The result was a policy that caused immense damage and hardship without good reason—never a sensible stance for a Leader to adopt, even one without democratic accountability.

The answer is not necessarily democracy. But it is, at least, a system efficacious enough to permit challenge. Even if you're the Leader of a country without a democratic tradition, surrounding yourself with good people willing to debate with you, and you being smart enough to realise the importance of being open to challenge, is an essential part of delivery. Without this, you may have the power to deliver, but you won't have the policy which, in fact, delivers.

China is very different from Russia in history, tradition, civilisation and in its bureaucracy. It may well possess within its system the capability to adjust and move from the present attempts to recreate a leadership of almost Maoist consolidation of power. And if it does, the reason will be precisely that such a consolidation, buttressed by ideological dispositions, will fail the delivery test.

Putin has had a major influence on the politics of the twenty-first century. There is indeed a sort of "Putin model" of governance. I remember when he started to crush nascent Russian democracy, turning elected positions into appointed ones, stripping out the sinews of a free media, casting political opponents as enemies of the nation, and being prepared even to eliminate some *pour encourager les autres.*

To begin with, people barely noticed, it seemed so discordant with the theory of the triumph of liberal democracy after the fall of the Soviet Union. When they did notice what was happening, Putin was viewed as an outlier, an exception, an example unlikely, so we thought, to be followed.

But many would-be Leaders were studying his trajectory, calculating whether it was indeed possible to concentrate absolute power in this way, crush dissent, and open up the prospect of a political longevity unthinkable in a genuine democracy.

They saw that it wasn't simply about the concentration of authority; it was also about developing a narrative as to why this was necessary in the interests of the country. And in a world changing fast, with economic and increasingly cultural insecurity, such a dominant authority figure seemed less frightening than the economic stasis and cultural relativism of traditional democratic Leaders.

The "strongman Leader" concept underwent a renaissance; and Putin was its exemplar.

In significant ways, there was alignment between the worries of the Western electorates and those supporting the emerging strongman Leaders in non- or quasi-democratic countries.

Both could see the world around them being changed in ways they didn't like and didn't feel they had consented to, both saw the authority figure as therefore their protection against this change, and neither believed that those opposing such figures had a viable plan for economic progress.

But above all, both believed that with the strongman, at least "something" would be done. The paralysis gripping democratic systems as they struggled with competing demands would be broken down by someone powerful enough, and indifferent enough to opposition, to do it.

This is why there is such ambivalence about Putin among both the far left and far right in democratic countries. His "admirers" are real.

There is much agonising as to how to arrest this anti-democratic trend.

What won't work are expressions of outrage which become ever more shrill, as it appears the outrage is not properly shared by other parts of the population.

What will work is comprehension as to the nature of the problem and the politics necessary to resolve it.

If you as a Leader don't recognise the people's anxieties and deal with them effectively, they will enable someone who does recognise them to take power, even if it means sacrificing traditional mechanisms of accountability. To take just one example: if you as a Leader don't comprehend the genuine concerns about rising immigration, the populist will quickly exploit your incomprehension.

In virtually every case, the populism is a response to the failure of conventional—what we might call "centrist"—politics to take strong positions which push back hard against the "deaf ear" tendency of elements of progressive politics.

There is no doubt in my mind that this represents a significant part of the appeal, enduring against all the odds, of Donald Trump in American politics.

When countries appear helpless on immigration, or weak in the face of extreme positions on culture war issues, we give sustenance to the populist.

This is another dimension of a failure to deliver. In this case, it is the perception that conventional politics is more interested in issues which, though important, don't impact the majority's everyday existence, but rather are driven by pressure from campaigning groups. The result is an impression that those in power don't have the time or the desire to focus on the things which really do affect people's daily lives.

The point from all this is that, as a Leader, you will have to focus on many different things. And in some countries, because of history or circumstances, maybe "delivery" is not the central thing. It could, in the moment, be about constitutional or institutional change. Or some aspect more to do with pure politics.

But, absent this, do not doubt for a single second, democracy or not or something in between, your task is to deliver.

CHAPTER EIGHT

The Supreme Importance of Strategy

The word "strategy" derives from the Greek *strategia*—generalship. Without it, there is no leadership.

It is one of my favourite political words. It implies clarity of thinking, coherence, cohesion, something which relegates the short term to its proper place and assists the long-term fulfilment of the overall plan.

Its presence does not guarantee success; but its absence pretty much guarantees failure.

Strategy is about keeping the day-to-day aligned with the year-to-year; making sure that the political necessities—or what seem necessities of the moment—do not collide with the strategic objectives of the government that define its essential purpose.

This is not a plan. It is an attitude. A state of mind. Like a computer chip, which sends a warning sign to the Leader whenever it looks like a decision is tactically right but strategically wrong.

This state of mind has to be developed before the Leader takes office. It must come with the Leader, part of their indispensable furniture when they enter office.

And the reason is that, after assuming power, the

Leader's life can evolve fast into a modus vivendi which constitutes a conspiracy against the identification and implementation of strategy.

I meet a lot of Leaders in the first flush of governing and they tend to go through exactly the same process I did. At first, things seem reasonably well ordered. You're giving instructions; the system is quite compliant; you have some political space; you may feel somewhat overwhelmed by the sense of responsibility, but you're not yet overwhelmed by the burden of governing.

Strategy seems to be present almost without volition because everything seems relatively calm.

Then slowly but with gathering speed the business of government comes upon you. Instruction gives way to the challenge of delivery; best intentions bump up against intractable realities; meetings, domestic and international, proliferate; the politics which seemed settled becomes turbulent. Suddenly the day gets so busy, the time for reflection shrinks; the resting time becomes disturbed.

Therefore, it is wise to be mentally prepared for the challenge of having an awareness of the importance of strategy and keeping to it. It is why, earlier, I spoke of the importance of the schedule. You need to carve out the periods of time when you and those closest to you can return constantly to the job of reconciling the day-to-day tactics to the core strategy.

The difference between "tactics" and "strategy" is fundamental.

Tactics are important. They help you deliver your plan.

Let's say a Leader needs a particular piece of legislation to pass. It is a major government reform. There are interests that may need assuaging, even buying off; there could be a tactical retreat on a certain non-vital part of it, to smooth its passage; or a special one-off alliance to secure the crucial goal of reform. All this is "tactics." Very necessary but all done in pursuit of the strategic objective.

But if the retreat is on a signal part of the legislation, the assuaging undermines the purpose of legislating, or strategic failure is the price paid for a temporarily easier life, then don't do it. The momentary comfort will result in prolonged discomfort when the account of government achievement arrives.

The confusion of tactics and strategy is one of the principal reasons why Leaders fail. They face a crisis. They take a measure to avert it. The measure meets the moment. But it collides with the politics of the final goal. Result: incoherence. The plan shrivels. The people lose confidence. The government takes a step closer to losing power.

The recent cost of living crisis that engulfed governments around the world is a case in point. Soon into the crisis, caused principally by external factors—energy crunch, war, etc.—it became clear that the sheer scale of the rise in gas prices was so steep that governments would have to bear a lot of the bill. The governments which came through it best were those that took measures—albeit unprecedented and costly—which at least to a significant degree aligned with their overall strategic objectives. For example, those combining subsidy with incentives to reduce energy demand, reform the long-term energy market and help meet climate targets. Those that just bunged money at the problem without strategic thought found the bills unaffordable and retreat without cohesion inevitable.

Once this starts to happen with a government, it is usually the beginning of the end—because the system begins to act randomly and so the tactics masquerading as strategy, but in fact denoting its absence, multiply. Incoherence begets incoherence. The people lose faith. Direction is lost and policies start to look like a set of individual forays into bits of the policy undergrowth without any consistent connectivity to the ultimate destination.

The strategy should remain fixed; it's the tactics which should alter. Flexibility with the latter; steadfastness with the former. Usually.

As ever, with the rule comes an exception. Things can happen, often external events the Leader has little control over, which change the foundational facts the strategy is based on.

At the turn of the twenty-first century Leaders in Europe generally believed that the era of big power conflict was over. Building up of armed forces had limited political purchase, and listed quite low on most governments' priorities. Then came Russia's invasion of Ukraine. Policy changed. Defence strategy changed. Because the facts upon which previous strategy was based also changed.

In the case of Ukraine, this change was so dramatic and vivid, it didn't take huge political discernment to spot it and to adjust strategy accordingly.

Sometimes, however, it is harder to identify when

something has shifted—not the surface issues but the fundamentals. I was sometimes too slow to spot such instances.

An interesting example, which shows how strategy should always be kept under review, is the relevance to economic growth of a modern industrial strategy.

The conventional wisdom when I was in office was that governments should steer clear of anything resembling "picking winners," as in a government trying to direct a particular industry or interfering with the generally smooth running of the market. France was considered an outlier in its "industrial champions" strategy, and there was a view that that strategy was not necessarily one to be emulated.

As with so much else, the technology revolution requires a reconsideration of this strategy of strict separation between market and government. Not a return to old-style "industrial strategy," which meant propping up industries which needed market-driven reform, but a recognition that without government taking a lively interest in how certain sectors of vital strategic importance are supported, the country will be less economically powerful and therefore the people poorer.

In Britain's case, this might mean supporting life sciences, and making sure the country retains its strong position in the strategically vital sector of AI.

In the case of France, it might be about attracting foreign investment, particularly in the financial sector where Brexit has given Paris an opportunity.

In the USA, a strategic industrial policy has led to a massive boost to green energy and industry.

All over Africa, countries are shaping up to reform their

agricultural sectors; trying to ensure the industrialisation of their raw commodities to which they need desperately to add value, rather than shipping the commodities out to other countries who gain that value.

These are all positions which the previous governments of those countries might have shied away from, or ignored. As circumstances change, however, so too should strategy.

So be firm in the adherence to strategy. But not rigid. John Maynard Keynes's saying that "when the facts change, I change my mind" remains a very sensible adage for Leaders to live by. It's important to note, however, that this is the amendment of strategy not the discarding of it. It doesn't mean yielding up the basic principle: keep strategic coherence; don't make the short term the enemy of the long term.

When Germany committed to the shutdown of its nuclear power sector following the 2011 Fukushima nuclear reactor accident in Japan, it met the prevailing public sentiment on nuclear energy. But fast-forward a decade and with the energy crisis and climate obligations, the tactical decision has collided with the strategic necessity of protecting living standards and reducing emissions.

All these questions of strategy require careful analysis, deep thought and constant reassessment. The challenge for the Leader is to remain on top of the strategic while battling the day-to-day.

On the day, the issues that dominate the headlines will seem the only things that matter, and the temptation will be huge to do whatever settles them in that moment of time.

Follow that course without regard to the long-term strategic consequence, and, yes, at the end of that day, you will heave a sigh of relief. But at a later date you will rue that decision, and shake your head in regret. Because it will inhibit, possibly fatally, your capacity to be a change-maker.

CHAPTER NINE

Be a Change-maker, Not a Place-holder

You're put in a position of leadership to make decisions. These can be decisions of commission. They can also be decisions of omission: when a Leader decides not to decide, that is still a decision, with consequences. Drift is a policy. It's just that it's not a very good one.

When I visited Shimon Peres—Israel's extraordinary prime minister, president and general political philosopher— he told me of a conversation he'd had with one of his successors when he saw him in the prime minister's official residence in Jerusalem. The successor was hesitating over how best to handle the peace process. Shimon finally said to him: "Look, you have a choice: you are here in this famous address as Leader of the country. Do you want to be in the history book or the visitors' book?"

If you're satisfied with the status quo as a Leader, you're unusual. Most Leaders have attained that position precisely by attacking the status quo. They also know that they were elected for a reason—to change people's lives for the better.

In any case, political inactivity is scarcely an option in a world that is changing so fast—indeed one that is character- ised by the scope, scale and speed of change. When I was prime minister, Twitter (or X) didn't exist, I had no mobile phone (something for which I have always, in retrospect, been grateful), the internet was if not in its infancy in its adolescence, Amazon was simply an online bookshop, Netflix hadn't been heard of; but more important, artificial intelligence was a concept not a revolution in progress, climate change was still hotly disputed, China was very much a developing nation, the Gulf countries mere petro-states, Britain a leader in Europe, Russia part of what was then the G8, India considered "Third World," and the USA embroiled in the post-9/11 fight against global jihadism.

At the turn of the millennium, the top ten companies in the world by market capitalisation comprised Microsoft, General Electric, Cisco, Walmart, Exxon, Intel, NTT Docomo, Royal Dutch Shell, Pfizer and Nokia. Today only one of those organisations—Microsoft—makes the list, which now boasts such enterprises as Apple, NVIDIA and Amazon.

Technology companies dominate, with market caps far in excess of the largest companies twenty years ago.

It's a new world! With all the challenges and opportunities novelty on this scale brings.

So, if you as a Leader are not a change-maker in such a world, it is you who are likely to be changed.

The Covid-19 crisis brought this lesson home, even if most people didn't think to analyse it in this way.

Just reflect on it. We had the modern world's first global pandemic. Tragically, it killed millions of people. It infected billions. And it shut the world down for a time. Yet ultimately, we came through it, the economy recovered far better than anyone might have anticipated, so did most of those who got sick, and we learnt a slew of lessons which should help us get through the next pandemic faster and with less pain.

Don't misunderstand me. I know that Covid is still circulating, the threat of new variants remains, the long Covid effects are still being worked out. But compare where we are to where we might have been, and what should impress us is our capacity for adaptation and survival, not our propensity for disaster.

How did we do this? We invented vaccines in record time, including those under the hitherto unheard-of nomenclature of mRNA, manufactured them, distributed them and—yes, albeit with much shameful inequality along the way—got them into the arms of more than half the world's population. Today there is the prospect of a whole new generation of vaccines and preventive injectables with the potential to save tens of millions of lives from communicable and non-communicable disease.

We created tests that worked in minutes to gauge infectiousness. We developed genomic sequencing which should allow us to build an early warning system to spot new pathogens, as well as in the longer term revolutionising diagnostics not only in medicine and disease detection but in agricultural production and beyond.

We couldn't mix socially during the pandemic. So, we resorted to Zoom. We couldn't work in the office. So, we worked from home. In the process we found not only that working in this way was feasible but that there were even some advantages to it. Of course, we all wanted lockdowns to end, but we kept going. And in the handling of the crisis, science and technology sprinted ahead in ways we did and did not expect.

The lessons of the Covid experience for governing are immense: urgency begat effectiveness, necessity begat inventiveness, desperation begat an upending of traditional silos and bureaucracy in government. We all displayed the capacity to change swiftly.

This was in a sense "wartime." But though the pressure on government to be as radical diminishes in peacetime, the fact of change does not. It is happening all the time. Government needs to acknowledge that fact. If the world around you is moving forward, and you're standing still, you get left behind.

So, all this is to emphasise: you should be a change-maker, not a place-holder.

Change, usually by way of reform, is in the circumstances of today almost akin to a duty. But it's also, unfortunately, the hardest thing to do.

The problem is that everyone nods in agreement when you talk about reform in principle; they just think it should apply to someone else.

In government, I was always trying to make reforms. And over time, I learnt that the process of reform has a certain rhythm to it. When you first propose a reform, people tell you it's a bad idea; when you're doing it, it's hell; and after you have done it, you wish you'd done more of it.

No change worth making comes without pain. Throughout the process, therefore, you will encounter resistance. It must be met with persistence.

Persistence, however, has to be combined with hard-headed realism. Try to change a whole system at once and you will probably fail. Make change step by step. That doesn't mean the change is not at each step radical; just that if you try to get to the destination point in a rush, those opposing it will find it easier to mobilise and will use the pain of upheaval to demonstrate that the whole reform project is flawed.

It's also important to create a constituency for the change. The benefits may lie a considerable way off and their full extent be unknown, but some people at least will be brave enough to acknowledge what might be achieved, some will understand that the change is actually to their advantage, and, if properly courted, some will come to see themselves as joint stakeholders vested in the reform.

To win converts, communicate the reform in language and terms the public will relate to. Weave it into the narrative for the government. Iterate and reiterate its purpose and its meaning. You're a Leader, not a technocrat. So, couch the message not in the form of summarising the functional things the reform will achieve, important though those are, but as underpinning the values you as a Leader believe in, the reason you sought the position of leadership. In other words, show how the change fits with the grand scheme of things, the plan. Don't simply recite the factual details.

The best reforms are those which become self-sustaining— that is, they don't need the Leader or the government to be constantly on the case because, once done, the reform has injected an agent of change into the system which has its own momentum independent of government oversight.

Governments are not great engines of innovation. They can innovate but they're not perpetually innovating. They can create but then they regard the job as done. They can, with the right leadership, change the status quo. But then there is a new status quo.

Or they begin but get diverted. Or the people charged with the reform change. Or the focus dissipates. A thousand different things.

So, ideally, you should make a reform that, once made, allows those empowered by it to take charge. Because, chances are, they won't be diverted.

Let me illustrate these various points by reference to the reforms my government made in education and healthcare. At the heart of the reforms was the idea of putting the parent/pupil and the patient first; i.e., consumer not producer interests.

For education that meant allowing schools independence from local government control, enabling them to form partnerships with the private sector, and giving them much greater freedom to hire and manage staff as they saw fit. So far as parents were concerned, they were empowered to choose a school for their children, if they felt the nearest one was giving a poor service.

This was particularly important in inner cities. In Hackney in East London, schools went from around 20 per cent of youngsters achieving the necessary grades at sixteen to over 80 per cent; and in another London borough one of the state schools last year sent more of their students to Oxford and Cambridge Universities than Eton.

For healthcare, in the UK's National Health Service, the

reform gave patients a choice as to health provider and brought private sector providers into the provision of NHS services.

Both reforms were met with significant hostility, from teachers on the one hand and the medical profession on the other.

During my first term in office, I tried whole-system reforms—performance-related pay for teachers, for example, and targets for doctors and hospitals. They didn't really work. During my second term, we adopted a different approach. We aimed for systemic, structural reform, but began in a limited way and built up our reforms over time. So, for example, we created academy schools—rather like charter schools in the USA—but began with just a few in those inner-city areas that were worst provided for. When it came to healthcare reform, we got the private sector involved to help bring down the long waiting lists for basic orthopaedic operations in the NHS. It was reasonably simple to do and was hard to resist.

These reforms became agents of change. As people saw schools improving and hospital waiting lists coming down, more of them came to support what was being done and, as time went on, to do so with increasing confidence and vigour. We were careful, though, to combine reform with investment in the basic infrastructure—school buildings and new health centres. It wasn't all pain for the system.

I fear that, too often, we failed to express our reforms in big-picture language and that we were too technocratic. But when we did it well, we reframed the argument not just in terms of the practical achievements of the changes, but in how they reflected a commitment to social justice. Good education and healthcare had largely been the prerogative of the well-to-do. Now, we said, both were available to the majority of the population dependent on state provision.

Today, the technology revolution offers further springboards and opportunities for reform. In healthcare, it promises to transform diagnostics and treatment, giving patients vastly improved control of their own conditions, using data to manage healthcare systems more efficiently, and reinventing life science. In education, it offers the prospect of bringing the best teachers in the world into the classroom and allowing pupils to learn at the pace most suited to them. The curriculum, concepts of class sizes, the role of the teacher, all have the potential to be radically changed through technological progress.

In the public sector more broadly, there are opportunities for biometric ID to enable interaction with government online; advances in DNA and facial recognition to improve law and order; not to mention transformation in the efficacy of everything from government procurement and smart cities to energy consumption and electric vehicles.

Sometimes when I talk with front-line politicians today, I find they're extraordinarily pessimistic about the possibilities of change. The money has run out, the politics is tough, the systems seem bolted into the edifice of government, impervious to change, and it all seems a little overwhelming.

I say, in response, this is an exciting time to be in government. The potential for change, the necessity of it in fact, is enormous. And so are the instruments, particularly in technology, at your disposal. It just requires the study to work out what those instruments are and the courage to take them in hand and use them.

Being a change-maker has never been more important, but also never been more achievable. So, go to it!

If you're not a change-maker in the circumstances of today, you are a place-holder, and pretty soon everyone will know that.

It will be tough, but if you don't step up to the challenge, the visitors' book is where you will end up!

CHAPTER TEN

Le Suivi: Delivering

Accepting it's all about delivery is not the same as delivering. The first is about understanding that "delivery" is the supreme political test; the second is understanding how to do it. Guess which is harder.

One of the most disconcerting lessons I learnt early in government was that, although I had a lot of power as prime minister, having the power and being able to exercise it were two different things.

When I sat for the first time in the prime minister's chair at the Cabinet table in Downing Street (the only chair with arms to it), I naively assumed that if I decided something, then that "something" would happen. My decision would be transmitted through the faithful system and its substance and intent faithfully implemented.

To my shock and discomfort, I realised, over time, that this was a serious misconception. Very often, nothing would happen. The "system" would learn of the decision, consider it, play around with it, have a vague stab at implementing it (on a good day), absorb it—and then bury it.

To be fair, this was not purely because the system was resistant to change.

More fundamentally and simply, it was because change is very difficult to make. It requires, as we have seen, good policy work and able personnel. It also requires a system that is geared to, focused upon and relentlessly pursuing delivery.

Thus, I became obsessed with what the French call *le suivi*. The follow-through. The move from vision to policy to implementation.

I mentioned earlier how in my second term in office we reorganised Downing Street and the centre of government to create more effective systems to deliver on core priorities. One of those creations was the Delivery Unit. It was an innovation so successful that it is now copied around the world by governments seeking to improve execution at the centre and often within particular ministries. Versions of it are advocated by consulting firms such as McKinsey.

As I said in Chapter 1, some things that government decides to do, while they may be complex at multiple levels politically, are relatively simple to carry out once agreed. They're a matter of legislation or of administrative diktat—the decision is the implementation, as it were. So, for example, when we introduced the minimum wage in the UK, we had to get the measure through Parliament, but once agreed it was done. Tick. Or take public sector worker pay. You want to increase it? You make the decision. It's done.

Where the challenge comes is when your decision involves deep systemic change. In part, this is because vested interests in embedded systems get in the way. But it's also because change of a systemic nature is genuinely complex. Reform of health, education or legal systems; welfare or subsidy payments; immigration and asylum processes;

digitisation of government; spreading the use of technology solutions in the public sector—these are all obvious to try, but, as experience shows, difficult to do. They involve grappling not just with "what" is to be done but "how" it is to be done, and the "how" often involves a degree of technical knowledge of which civil servants and their political masters have, at best, only a limited understanding.

Those countries that tried using their own government health experts to create a Covid vaccine almost universally failed. Those like the USA and the UK who put the private sector in charge succeeded.

Think of all those extraordinary NASA space missions. Amazing work. Brilliant science. But it took Elon Musk to revive the industry and make spacecraft reusable thus slashing what were otherwise unaffordable costs.

There is a reason why the Soviet five-year plans basically failed. The failure was inherent. There was determination to meet a target but no ingenuity in achieving it and no flexibility to alter it.

Implementation depends on the support and cooperation—or at least acquiescence—of many actors. It requires breaking down the different components of the change, understanding all the different dimensions of it, and—vital—tracking that what is supposed to happen does, in fact, happen.

The private sector is familiar with such processes and tends to be better at them. But, then, to be frank, it's easier for the non-state sector. Yes, there are special interests that resent or oppose change, and employees who are resistant to it, but, in the end, the leadership will get what it wants, the market will likely be pushing it, and there's no politics to get in the way. If the managers get things wrong or have to abandon the change, they will be sacked, the company will lose money or go out of business. For governments, the ability to cancel or change course is harder, and the cost of failure much higher.

I always say to business people who complain about the processes of government: come and try it—it's a darn sight harder than you think.

Hence the Delivery Unit, which was born out of the belief, based on my experience during my first term in office, that we needed something constructed specifically to deal with this challenge of implementation.

Over time we learnt how to make it work most effectively. And now, with my institute's experience in helping set up Delivery Units all over the world, we can see there are certain clear rules as to how such units should be established and how to make them function.

Foremost among these is the vital importance of choosing a limited number of priorities the unit should focus on—the priorities being those things the Leader most cares about. That stump speech I wrote about earlier where the Leader imagines what they want to list as achievements when seeking re-election, or leaving office for that matter, those are the things the Delivery Unit should be tasked with.

This point needs to be emphasised. I sometimes come across governments whose Delivery Unit is effectively a planning ministry for the whole government. It never works. The Delivery Unit is not meant to shadow the government. It is a focused, targeted, laser-beam-like instrument of delivery of the Leader's priorities. And only works as such.

Those priorities should be measurable, as objectives and key results (OKRs) are in the private sector. If you can't measure it, forget it—at least for Delivery Unit purposes. A goal of reducing poverty or providing jobs for the youth? That's too vague. A specific poverty reduction programme or youth employment policy with specific targets for delivery? Yes, that works.

We used the Delivery Unit to reduce waiting lists for hospital treatment, to cut unjustified asylum claims, to deliver the schools reform programme. These were all measurable reforms. Success was clear. Failure couldn't be concealed.

It's also essential that the Leader is personally and intimately involved in the work of the Delivery Unit, that the system knows its authority is vested in him or her, and that if the system offends the unit, it knows it is offending the Leader. When the Delivery Unit picks up the phone to talk to a ministerial department, or even a minister, the recipient of the call must know that they're speaking to the source of power and not merely to a functionary. This cannot be done through assertion. It is done by demonstration and example.

While I was prime minister, I ran a session every month for each of the unit's priorities—at which the relevant government minister would be present—where the Delivery Unit team would make a presentation that set out what progress had, or hadn't, been made on the particular priority. I did this not only because I wanted to know what was happening, but because I wanted to demonstrate that the priorities were mine, that they were owned by me, and that the unit was doing my bidding and was accountable to me.

Presentations were carefully structured: priority, progress, problems, path through them.

Those who serve in the Delivery Unit have to be chosen with enormous care. As a rule, outsiders with specialist knowledge should be part of the team. Of course, there's a strong risk that they will be treated with suspicion by the insiders, but working with the system but not formed by it, they will hugely improve delivery capacity.

General suspicion is, in any case, inevitable, at least at first. Ministers and ministries will view the Delivery Unit as an interference from the centre—an unnecessary irritation at best, a threat at worst. In time, if things are managed properly, they will come to see it as an aid, an advantage, an additional reinforcing mechanism of their own position, and they can also bask in the delivery success. But to begin with, they will be wary.

One key priority for the Delivery Unit function is to assemble the right data. Get the facts, I would always say. The ministries will tell you "Don't worry, everything is fine, it is on track." By the time you find out it isn't so, it will be too late. So, part of the Delivery Unit's job is to search out the truth, leave no stone unturned, no obstacle hidden or unaddressed.

That's no easy task. Situational unawareness, as I found, especially after 9/11 when we were scrambling to protect the nation's security and to engage with different countries and cultures, can be a chronic limitation on efficacy, appreciated too late.

However, it matters in the more mundane terrain of systemic reform of services, too. The Leader needs to know the situation on the ground, to have first-hand awareness of the challenges the services are struggling with, and not to assume they know but to be confident that they do. The Delivery Unit should be the forager after the reality, the real-world link between the government and the governed.

Lastly, to lead a government you have to know what the government you're leading is doing—or not doing! Preparing for Prime Minister's Questions was a slog, but the one benefit was you discovered a great deal about what was happening beneath you. Supposedly under your leadership. And some of it was horrifying. Bits of bureaucracy gone mad. Policies that some bright spark had decided would light up their ministry, of which you were completely unaware.

The Delivery Unit function is to make you aware that what you want done is being done, and to give you a mechanism to correct course if delivery goes awry.

Across government, the same mentality should prevail. What is true for the Leader—prime minister or president— should be true for the departments under them. Ministers also should know their priorities (hopefully aligned roughly with the Leader's) and be similarly focused on implementation.

In every organisation, the toughest task is turning promise into proof.

CHAPTER ELEVEN

Sugaring the Long-term Changes: Quick Wins

The problem with long-term change is just that: it's long term and politics and politicians tend to have short-term horizons. In a democracy, there are elections and election cycles; and even when the people aren't electors, or not in a serious competitive sense, they are still "the people."

Most long-term gain is via short-term pain. It usually involves structural reform. It means taking on established systems, vested interests and, almost invariably, has its losers who can immediately identify themselves and its winners who can't, but who are the unnamed beneficiaries of the future when the reform has materialised. The former shout loudly; the latter stay silent.

There is no real achievement in government without such change because the pain is the path to the gain; and often the more the pain, the more the gain, because the change is large in scope and fundamental in effect.

I say to the presidents and prime ministers I work with: start the process of long-term reform early because it likely will not yield results until near the end of the first term.

However, many reforms will not come through even after your first term has expired. If you're lucky enough to get another term, you will see the benefit practically and politically.

But of course, you still have to get through that first term, and that is the worry for Leaders.

Hence you need to sugar the pill, which means you need to look for where and how you get the "quick wins." There is nothing more sure to make a politician's ears prick up than discussion of "quick wins." About the earliest lesson in the harsh realities of governing is that the people's expectations run far ahead of any mortal's ability to deliver. So within a terrifyingly short timescale, people begin to moan: you promised change, but I see no sign of it; you said you would transform the country, but my life is still shit; it's always jam tomorrow and I want some today; you politicians are all the same; etc., etc., etc., as Yul Brynner said in the musical *The King and I*.

It's all unreasonable and reasonable at the same time. It's reasonable to expect that a politician winning an election on the basis of change will make the change. And it's unreasonable to think it can arrive fast. The expectation is understandable and the reality irrefutable. But then, that's why politics is a tough business.

So, you need to effect some change quickly enough to keep the hope up. A "quick win" is one that comes in a year, max two. It gives you a sliver of achievement to lay before the impatient to prove that in time it's just possible more will come. It's a persuader of good intentions; an earnest of trust.

It's nothing to be overly proud of: the long-term structural change is the matter of pride. But it's a necessary short-term tactic for the survival essential to deliver the long term.

Quick wins come in many shapes and sizes. But the characteristics they share are that they have impact, in a circumscribed timescale, in a manner which the people notice, and in a form through which they subscribe the win to the Leader.

They can be purely political: the removal of some hated institution or law; the appointment of a credible anticorruption tsar; the embrace of a former political opponent to demonstrate national unity. These are political signals, indicating a different approach, set of values, order of priorities. They're effective to a degree, but the risk is that because they're not "daily life" things, they can often appeal more to the political elite than the real people.

They can be a well-targeted expenditure of money. I am well aware that spending money is the easiest thing in government and the least politically courageous. Basically, any idiot can do it. However, doing it in a way that doesn't clash with the long-term changes; that makes the largesse vaguely proportionate to the affordability from the point of view of the country's finances; that reaches the right people, and makes a difference in their lives—that is a skill. India's prime minister Narendra Modi's promise of proper toilet access for all was a classic example. Easy to grasp; big in effect; and because of the sanitation implications, sensible long term.

It could be a new road in a rural area or improved access to electricity—bearing in mind that approximately a third of African homes are without it. Now, the advent of satellite technology, which for rural areas is much more effective than cable, to bring the internet within reach of every community, is a great quick win for Leaders, as my institute is proving in a growing number of countries all over the world.

Technology is the new field of quick wins. Digitising government services; cutting out the middleman in any state payments by digital transfer; creating new apps—for rural farmers, for example. Even introducing a digital ID or smart health card can ensure recognition that things are changing and can be done in half of a term of government.

The best things therefore are either physically tangible—you can touch them, see them, feel them; or virtually tangible. Whichever way, the impact is undeniable. That is why Leaders traditionally went for infrastructure projects. They're a physical reality. You just have to make sure that they are the right projects, and they make a difference to the right people in the right places. And now their virtual equivalents can be just as big a "quick win" and sometimes better and faster.

If possible, avoid subsidy, or at least the old-fashioned simple bung or sweetener. The problem with subsidies is they're popular for sure; but they're virtually impossible to take away even if the costs then spiral or the original justification declines in significance. And at some point, someone—the IMF for example—will come along and tell your public it's a really bad idea.

Best of all is when the win symbolises and enriches the basic narrative of the government. We did this when we introduced the minimum wage. It worked at every level. It was beneficial; it was affordable; and most of all it symbolised a new approach, with different and better values.

When you come into government, don't assume that the best "quick wins" are the ones you conceived of in opposition. Take your time. Not too long naturally, but long enough that when you have looked under the hood of government and seen what is possible, you have an informed idea of what is quick and what is a win.

Finally, though you shouldn't be too excited about what is, in the end, a mere tactic, don't be so purist as not to do it. You need quick wins. You need something to talk about that is plain, simple and popular. The rest of your government needs it.

For governments in the developing world, who receive support from the international donor community, there is an important avenue of opportunity to secure some quick wins without damaging the already fragile public finances. It is worth spending some time and energy thinking about what the donors would support, and seeing if a quick win can be tailored around it. The donor community responds far better to clear, worked-out plans which, preferably, mean that they also participate in the righteous glow from the "win." So, fashion them accordingly.

Done well, the quick wins give you breathing space for what really matters: changes that mean the next generation does better than the current one, and the future is brighter than the past; changes that demonstrate that politics done well alters the lives of the people for the better.

But these are the hard ones.

CHAPTER TWELVE

Nothing Is Inevitable in Politics, Neither Defeat nor Victory

Often, I hear politicians or commentators talk of the political fortunes of a party or a person as certain. Certain to fail. Certain to succeed.

There is no such thing.

Of course, there are probabilities. There are likely outcomes. If you're trailing 20 points in the polls and there is a short time until an election, you will look like you're beaten. Or 20 points ahead and you will look like you're in. For sure.

Except that nothing is for sure in politics.

The interesting question is: if it seems as if defeat or victory beckons, what can the Leader do to avoid the one and secure the other?

Let's assume you're staring at defeat.

First work out the reasons why. This can be harder than you think, because those around you and possibly you yourself may well have sunk into delusion or denial. Work out what's really at the bottom of people's predilection for your opponents or more pertinently their disdain for you.

The British Labour Party's history is unfortunately an object lesson in the power of self-deception. As its recent history shows.

It lost in 2010 (though no party commanded a majority), because it moved somewhat but enough from being New Labour to be too much like Old Labour. It lost in 2015 (giving the Conservative Party its majority), because it had moved sharply left. It then suffered a monumental defeat in 2019 because it had moved ultra left.

At each stage, it swallowed the extraordinary proposition that the people were voting Tory because Labour was insufficiently left wing. Quite why the British people should have behaved so irrationally was never explained. But the belief in this delusion was absolute—as it had been in the 1970s and 80s and even to a degree in the 1990s.

Only now has the Labour Party, thankfully for those who need it, come to its senses under new and effective leadership.

The Conservatives will eventually rue the time they allowed Euroscepticism, in a perversion of Thatcherism, to dominate their party. They could have won all the last elections without it; and finally, they will lose power for longer than they need because of it.

So, confronting why you're doing badly requires a clear-headed analysis of what's bugging the people about you, which can't be put to one side for reasons of difficulty, sensitivity or, least of all, ideology.

If you're in opposition, this ought to be reasonably straightforward, though it is extraordinary how regularly oppositions confuse the world as it is with the world as they wish it to be.

If you're in government, it can be more tricky. Governments can be unpopular when doing "the right thing."

Reforms will be hated while in progress. Leaders can be measured against unreasonable standards of perfection as the nation vests its hopes in them. Public sentiment can be swayed by a succession of scandals or bad news.

You then have to measure not just the breadth but the depth of this feeling, quality as well as quantity. Opinion polls are snapshots. Significant but still only that. How firm the numbers are is a whole other thing. People might answer the polling question by giving the answer they think they should give, not necessarily what they truly believe, or the answer that recent negative coverage suggests. But none of this goes deep. A puff of wind can unsettle it.

The fundamentals, though, may be different. And they do go deep. Has the government got a plan? Is it acting, even if unpopularly, strategically? And, of course, is it delivering? What do people really think? And I mean real "people," those who are not political activists, who don't feel strongly about politics, who don't devour the news schedules, who don't listen to political podcasts, who don't talk about politics at the dinner table, i.e., THE MAJORITY.

They ask a very simple question as the day of judgement approaches: what's best for me and my family?

That's why the famous catchphrase in the Clinton campaign for the American presidency, "It's the economy, stupid," is so frequently cited. Because it's basically true. If security is at risk, that may trump it, of course. But by and large, people vote without reference to ideology according to their immediate interests: what will make their children and them better off, more prosperous.

Crime, public services, health, education, transport all

feed into this, of course, but in the end, they matter because they affect that crucial sense of well-being. Better off is not just about the money in people's pockets but about the quality of life as it is affected by those things for which government is responsible.

A credible economic offer of hope for a better future is preconditional. Without it, you lose. And I think that is for sure.

And it is an essential component of a campaign for re-election.

Re-election begins with a focus on what the priorities will be for the next term in office.

"Mantra" is a word originally found in Hinduism and Buddhism, meaning either the thought behind an action or something repeated continually to aid concentration. And I always say a good mantra to think about for re-election is: A LOT DONE; A LOT TO DO; A LOT TO LOSE.

A LOT DONE is a claim of achievement necessary to support the idea you have not been wasting the people's time during the existing mandate.

A LOT TO DO is an acknowledgement: you haven't met all the expectations, and recognise the task ahead, but know what it is.

A LOT TO LOSE is a warning: vote for the other lot and what has been gained up to now will be lost.

The first is boastful without the humility of the second. The second is an admission of failure without the first. The last is a reminder to the people that the standard they should apply is one of choice not perfection.

You need them all together.

I remember just before my first re-election campaign, when we were ahead in the polls and frankly coasting a little, taking a call from Bill Clinton, recently retired as president. "How are you doing?" he asked. "Oh, fine," I replied; "you know, we're explaining all the things we've done, reciting the achievements." "Hmm," he said; "well, in that case they may just say thank you very much and goodbye."

The point he was making—which correctly shook me out of coasting mode—is that it is always about the future and therefore simply saying what you have done is not enough unless you spell out what you still have to do, which is the reason you are asking people to re-elect you.

It's better if your party is united. But it's a myth that a divided party is bound to fail. It is never division in itself that causes defeat but division that obscures direction. In other words, provided the Leader is in charge and capable of exerting authority and giving clarity of direction, the fact they have those within the ranks who are in disagreement will ultimately not prevent victory. But if the division is one which they look incapable of resolving in the manner the leadership wants, so that there is neither the sense of the Leader in charge nor the clear direction, that is fatal.

When leading the Labour Party, I had plenty of people who were forever disagreeing, speaking out, complaining. But the public knew I was in control. In fact, at points, the disagreements were helpful since they underlined the degree to which the control was being exercised.

So, all those qualities described in the previous chapters— strategy, having a plan, focus on delivery, strength as

93

Leader—if you can find the time, the intelligence and the energy to embrace them, things can always be rescued.

It won't happen without them; but with them, particularly if you can draw a contrast with your opponent, you have a fighting chance, and that's as good as it gets in politics.

What is the problem? What is the solution? The deep problem, the deep solution.

If you do this with no holds barred, delusions scattered, details accounted for, embracing even the most painful awareness, you can still pull it back.

Conversely, you can be ahead, and all may still be lost. If the probable victory is based on transient negativity for your opponents, sentiments which don't run deep, and your policies are partially but not completely ready, your weaknesses not remedied because mistakenly you think the lead is so comfortable you don't need to remedy them, or you haven't planned the strategy with the precision required, well, you can end up with a nasty shock.

One president I worked with—a good guy, who had won twice—was sure that he could choose his successor and get him elected. The polls were favourable. The president's own standing, if not stellar, was reasonable.

But if he had taken a step back and analysed the situation, he would have recognised that the would-be successor was old and not energetic, that his programme was lacklustre, and that his opponent was vigorous and promising change.

There wasn't a strategy, a plan or strength in execution. Come polling day, the lead evaporated.

There was another important lesson from that campaign which applies generally.

Never underestimate your opponent. Better, to a fault, to overestimate them. Treat them with respect. Work out their weaknesses but start by working out their strengths.

I remember when people on the progressive side of politics would disparage Ronald Reagan—"brainless," "superficial," "too old," "too folksy," etc.—and I would say, well, given he's beaten our side twice, what does that make us? You could ask the same question today of those who snorted with derision at Joe Biden before he won the presidential election in 2020.

If your opponent is a proven winner, assume they have something which has allowed them to win. If they're a contender and you don't believe in the inevitability of your victory, ask what their appeal is and how you counter it.

At regular junctures I have praised the necessity of staying cool, of dispassion. It's never more important than when contemplating supposedly sure-fire victory or defeat. You can always come back if you are clever enough to discover and chart the route; and you can always lose your way before the finishing line by being cocky, complacent or failing to go deep enough to see what brings that line into focus and within reach.

And if all that makes you anxious as a Leader, in this limited instance, that's an anxiety that's healthy.

PART III

Policy Lessons

CHAPTER THIRTEEN

Your First Duty: Keeping People Safe

As I've said before, it's a good rule of thumb when contemplating policy to start by thinking about yourself not as a politician but as a normal person. What do you want from government? Well, lots of things. Good economic policy; public services; some sort of attachment to decency and integrity. And so on. But the first thing you want to know is that it's going to try to keep you and your family safe.

If you don't feel safe, nothing else in your life is going to compensate for the absence of basic security.

Politicians, particularly from the progressive left, constantly underestimate this; or, even worse, sometimes seem to sympathise as much with the perpetrator of crime as the victim.

But, in my experience, ordinary law-abiding folk feel quite viscerally about crime and security. They dislike being threatened or feeling threatened.

Now, security can come in different forms—or rather the threats to it can do so.

There are the big macro security threats. There is the threat of invasion, or of actions by state or non-state actors. And then there are the threats of everyday criminality.

Obviously, they require very different responses and preparations. But the basic principle is the same: the first duty of government is to keep the people safe.

There has been a threat from extremism these last decades from Islamist jihadists and more recently from the far right. 9/11 changed security policy the world over. I know there is a common view that America overstretched to deal with the terrorist threat, but in the aftermath of the worst terrorist attack the world had seen, there was at the time not much support for understretch; and as I saw first hand, the American president and people were determined that the response be so overwhelming that no one would again attempt such an act.

Ukraine's fight against Russian aggression is not only to defend their country for today but to deter any possible repeat of that aggression in the future.

The actions against Tigrayan separatism in Ethiopia; the struggles against Boko Haram in Nigeria; the military campaign of Saudi Arabia and the UAE in Yemen: the point is not to debate the wisdom of the individual policy, but to emphasise that, for governments, controlling the security space is essential even if it means a fight on the country's own territory, even with its own people, even with its own neighbours.

One of the commonest threats today is from Islamist terrorism. Many countries face it. All try to overcome it, with varying degrees of success.

The reality is that if the government cannot properly deal with it, a country will be in trouble, destabilised and insecure. The people are distracted and worried, business feels nervous, society fractures, a country's progress is stalled at best and disintegrates at worst. People lose faith in the long term and therefore play for the short term only. No nation can prosper like that.

Right now, in the Sahel region of Africa, democracy is under siege because governments can't defeat the jihadist menace that flows down from Libya into that band of countries across northern sub-Saharan Africa; and from there it is seeping into West Africa and in East Africa from Somalia down the eastern coast.

The result is that the efforts at development of both the countries themselves and the international donor community are rendered much less impactful. Without security, development is impossible.

There is a common belief particularly among the NGO community that without development, security is at risk because, in the absence of hope of a better life, people turn to the solutions of the extremists. There is truth in this. And it is certainly correct that the extremists are adept at leaping on the back of local grievances and, a bit like Western populists, exploiting them.

However, while it is partially true, what is completely true is that if security dissolves, the chance of improvement and development dissolves with it. The coups which have removed governments across the Sahel were, in part, motivated by the failure of the democratically elected governments to perform that first essential duty. They couldn't keep the people safe. Security was more important to ordinary people than democracy.

Now, of course, it would have been better to have

retained democracy, particularly in a country like Niger whose president was genuinely trying to make effective change, and to have improved the security situation through reform with outside help and not through paramilitary organisations like the Wagner group from Russia.

But the point is once the security battle is lost, the faith of the population in change and the prospect of progress goes with it.

Against these large threats emanating from groups with links across the world, governments need systems of security in place which require: intelligence-gathering, surveillance, precision weaponry, strong command and control centres; in other words, whole-system effective government.

Developed countries have the capacity to do this. The developing world often struggles. It would be wise if the developed world did more to help those developing countries in need. Because, quite apart from everything else, if those countries begin to destabilise, their citizens start to contemplate searching for a better life, and that usually means heading to Europe or America. However, that is another topic.

The developing world is the site of most of the terrorist threats globally today. Almost certainly, these countries' conventional security forces will be inadequate, lacking both specialist training and equipment. The only way to correct this situation is therefore to bring help in from the outside. Many Western countries, like Britain and the USA and France, provide this help.

The point is: for the Leader faced with such a threat there is literally nothing more important than getting the means of defeating it. Don't be proud. Beg and borrow if you have to. Focus like a laser on it. Get your best people in charge of it. Find the best people anywhere you can to assist in making them better still. Mobilise the international community—the donors—to understand that if they're not helping you with this, it's no use them supporting a rural schools programme or smallholder farmers, because nothing else will work if security isn't working.

Mozambique has faced and is facing a jihadist threat in Cabo Delgado in the north of the country, where the country's enormous reserves of gas, crucial for economic development, are due to come on stream. The president was not afraid to ask for outside help as the country's forces struggled to get on top of the problem. As a result, the otherwise stalled gas project was renewed.

One final crucial point: your law enforcement agencies need to behave; need to have the discipline that, even when provoked, they don't mirror the conduct of the people they're fighting. So much damage is done when those supposed to uphold security start abusing their power, targeting "suspect" communities, heavy-handed at all times, not just when necessary.

This is much harder to accomplish than it sounds. Your security forces lose colleagues to the violence, they see atrocities, they become desperate in their desire to get results. But you must keep iron discipline, with commanders who understand that at least trying to bring local communities onside is a vital component of a strategy for success.

Security—the capacity to protect your country without and within—is number one. So if you come to power, and it is a problem, treat it like a crisis. Settle it before anything else.

More mundane but for normal life probably more important—in the developed world or stable developing nations anyway—is "law and order." In other words: protection from criminals and criminal behaviour.

I made my name on this issue as an aspiring Labour Leader. The Labour Party, like most of the left back in the 1990s, was thought to be "soft" on crime, keen to "blame" society, uncomfortable with ascribing individual responsibility, except in respect of white-collar crime, committed by "rich" people.

But I learnt two things about crime growing up. First, it is the poorest communities who suffer most from crime. They're the ones with the drug-dealers next door, the gangs running the neighbourhood, the fear of venturing out, the hassle and the humiliation at the hands of bad people, their children given the worst role models.

Second, stay on that word "humiliation" for a moment. To be powerless in the face of crime is humiliating. And that matters to people. I remember the guy who urinated against the door of a house in my street and then threatened me with a knife when I tried to stop him. These things stick with you because in some way they aren't just unpleasant but puncture your self-esteem.

I took up the issue of crime and made it a Labour issue. We say we represent the working people. So, represent them.

That, however, is just an attitude, if the right one. To deal with crime you need much more. Like everything else you need a strategy.

From my study of nations which have very low crime rates, it begins with culture. Zero tolerance is definitely right, in my view. Nothing that is bad behaviour affecting the peace of mind of the law-abiding should be tolerated.

In Western society today, we have decided, effectively, whatever language might be used from time to time by Leaders anxious to show they "get it," to tolerate quite a lot. In inner cities gang culture is rife. Drug-dealing usually goes unpunished. Organised crime finds it reasonably easy to flourish. Many cases of burglary are not investigated. Court systems are ludicrously out of date and slow. And then those criminals who do end up in prison are often in what are essentially schools of crime not rehabilitation.

When I was in power, I focused a lot of attention on this issue, and ours was the first government in Britain since the Second World War to see crime fall. With a degree of success, had it been built upon, we would have made big strides towards being a world leader for a reasonably large, developed nation on crime.

Obviously, a lot of developing countries are in a similar position, though there, given the lack of resources, it is more understandable.

The fact nevertheless remains that, whatever the individual circumstances of a nation, once a degree of tolerance for criminality takes hold, it creates a dangerous culture. The criminal element, or some of it, thinks it's untouchable. The public lose hope. The system gives up. Too many rules, bureaucratic form-filling, procedures, inquiries which never begin, processes which never end.

If it gets really bad, then the risk is that some new Leader will arrive on the scene and say: screw the system and the rules and the processes. I am going to take a hammer to this nut and crack it. And surprise surprise, the general public will say hallelujah. Think President Bukele and his anti-gang programme in El Salvador.

The point is you can't uphold due process, unless the process is seen to deliver justice. And that doesn't mean simply to the accused.

So, if you don't want policy driven to extremes, act. You don't have to rip up due process, but you may well have to change it. Start from the proposition that what is intolerable will not in fact be tolerated; and work back from that.

As with any other issue, deconstruct the system, analyse what is not working, and then set out to fix it. You will find an enormous list of things which don't work, unfortunately. And the fixing will be tough. The police and investigating authorities will likely need more powers; and the granting of those powers will be fiercely contested.

The court system may need a complete overhaul. Technology solutions—everything from DNA records to surveillance operations to financial monitoring—may require new legal frameworks and capability.

Like the bigger national security issue, your law enforcement officers must protect communities, not exploit them or engage in corruption. There has to be a level of trust between police and local communities for this to work. But, just to take Britain as an example, I can honestly say that in my forty years in British politics, I never met a community that wanted less policing.

And here is the unalloyed good news for the Leader:

tackling the challenge of "law and order" works electorally! Yes, believe it or not, people prefer to be safe.

Wherever I am in the world, I ask the Leader: what's the crime like here? Usually I get an immediate response, good or bad. But sometimes to my astonishment I can tell they haven't really thought about it.

Crime matters in many more dimensions than the obvious one of protecting society. Low crime is good for business. Someone is thinking of investing in your country. "Is it safe?" is one of the first questions! It's good for tourism. If you're choosing your holiday destination, guess which one you're not choosing. The one you just read about in the papers as the location of some horrendous crime.

And it says something important about your country. Something not just about its culture but about its spirit. Crime is not an issue in Singapore because the authorities decided it was not going to be. The methods were without doubt at times open to question, but a narrative about the country was created: crime wasn't going to be tolerated. Nothing stood in the way of that objective. This policy was not incidental to the success of Singapore, it was of the essence.

It was all about the leadership. As it always is.

CHAPTER FOURTEEN

Lessons for the Economy

Economies vary so much in nature that it seems counter-intuitive to imagine common lessons. What has the economy of the USA got to do with that of Sierra Leone? How do you compare China with Myanmar? History, scale, resources, culture, geographical position, state of development—all these distinguishing characteristics make it hard, at first blush, to understand how circumstances so different in each case can, nonetheless, yield shared teachings.

For sure, First World developed countries do have certain things in common, as do the world's poorest nations. But there are also more general discernible principles than we think, even if they don't all apply equally in all cases. It's therefore very instructive to examine how, over the past half-century, some countries have advanced in economic prosperity while others have declined.

If we look at the most notable cases of progress, we see, in each case, decisions that were taken and implemented which led to transformative change.

In the late 1970s and 80s China, after decades of a tightly managed Communist economy, opened up to international trade and investment. In 2001, it joined the World Trade Organization. No country in the globe's history has achieved such economic and material advance on such a scale over the course of thirty years. But it started with a decision of leadership.

South Korea built itself after a prolonged conflict which divided the Korean peninsula and its people, going through a period of corrupt regimes and military domination, until through leadership and reform it emerged in the twenty-first century as one of the world's economic powerhouses.

The countries of Eastern Europe joined the European Union and began some of the most remarkable political and economic reform in human experience. Poland—a country which struggled to shake off its Soviet shackles—has, through the reform programme demanded by the EU, become one of the wealthiest nations on the continent, with real wages rising in some years by almost 10 per cent.

The point is none of these stories is about chance or luck or some serendipitous event. Their success can be directly attributed to decisions of Leaders and governments.

I was prime minister of one of the world's largest economies. Since leaving office, through the Tony Blair Institute, I have worked with countries in the Gulf, in South East Asia, Eastern Europe and Africa whose economies vary hugely from that of the UK and from each other's. But there are clearly identifiable common features, lessons which apply— whatever the context, whatever the individual national characteristics—across cultures and in spite of multiple and diverse challenges.

First and foremost, all successful nations have sought, obtained and sustained macroeconomic stability. Fiscal and monetary policy has been pursued with consistency and obedience to the basic precepts of balancing accounts, affordable debt levels, keeping the currency honest, independent central banks (usually though not always), and the avoidance of uncalculated risk.

I have concluded that this is not a question of left vs right but right vs wrong. Good macroeconomic policy is a prerequisite of economic progress.

That is not to say there aren't big debates about individual policies. Post-financial crisis, some countries favoured monetary easing; some didn't. Some academics have proposed fiscal expansion to restore growth; some think that is injurious to long-term financial health. There is a wide range of views about the right macro policy to produce growth, about fiscal policy, about the point at which certain policies can put stability at risk.

But what is not in contention is that losing credibility in macro policy and thus endangering stability is fatal. Consistently maintaining confidence in an economy and therefore access to credit is a precondition of success.

Ultimately, if a government looks as though it can't pay its bills, it will be in trouble, as even a highly developed nation like the UK found to its cost in September 2022 when a mini-budget that sought to fund tax cuts through increased borrowing caused consternation in the markets. The credibility of a government, its finance ministry and central bank underpin the overall credibility of every country.

OK, that may seem obvious, but it needs stating because occasionally Leaders think they can play a bit fast and loose with this credibility. They can't.

Nations should be open to investment, both internal and external. No country succeeds without it. In my experience,

Leaders love it when people are investing in their country: it says something positive not just about the economy but the country itself.

So, when Leaders ask me how to attract investment—and they can be Leaders of countries with vast investment potential—I tell them the answer is simple: predictability and stability. But unfortunately, I often have to add, your country is a world away from either. You may think it isn't; and the system may tell you, the Leader, that it's geared to attracting the investment the country needs. But if you speak to your country's existing investors or those who might have an interest in investing, they will tell you the true state of affairs.

Creating a good business and investment climate is the swiftest way to attract capital: predictable rules, properly applied; contracts awarded without corruption. The challenge is that this generally involves reform of systems that have represented the precise opposite of those attributes. Changing the system requires cultural as well as regulatory changes. But there is no doubt what works. Any reasonably smart business leader or economist of international standing can tell you. The issue is whether you're listening!

Countries should be prepared to go out and showcase what they have: attach themselves to major investment conferences, hold special meetings for investors of interest. They should venture out into the world, not wait for people to turn up at their door.

They should also have a strong process in place for follow-up. Yes, *le suivi* matters here too. I often see countries getting encouraging initial interest from potential investors. Maybe the head of state personally meets them. There is real enthusiasm. But then it is passed down the ranks and disappears into the impenetrable morass of the bureaucracy. Having an investment or promotion agency or board, which focuses on identifying opportunities and how they might be accessed, is a good idea. However, such an agency will only work if it has the complete and demonstrated support of the Leader and possesses the power to act across government to shift obstacles.

Resist economic nationalism. By this I don't mean refuse to support national champions of proven excellence or discard industrial strategy. I mean don't make it hard for international companies who really can add value to your economy to enter on the fallacious grounds that you can do it on your own. Getting high-quality financial, intellectual and management capital into a country is an essential part of development.

Interesting side note: the UK's car industry only really revived after chronic decline in the 1970s when Nissan from Japan was allowed to set up its plant in the north-east. It showed the way to modern efficiency and the rest of the industry followed to significant and positive effect.

Nations that are rich in natural resources but export them unprocessed, allowing value to be added elsewhere, need to attract those investors who have a track record of value-added processing. Doing this is harder than it sounds but is possible if the country has a clear and plausible understanding of what is available and how an investor could exploit it, and is able to target investment to the individual companies that it believes will add value.

My institute has helped secure some major investments from large international firms in countries with a poor record of processing their raw material—like cotton or other crops. These firms carry out the necessary processing or manufacturing locally, so that at least some of that substantial added value is kept in the country that produces it.

There are, however, still examples of countries that grow substantial crops but export them unprocessed to other more developed nations, with the finished product from their crop coming back as expensive imports. Crazy. And, of course, very bad for balance of payments.

For developing countries especially, I favour an industrial strategy approach. Work out a coherent plan of what you have, what its potential is, how it might relate to the other things in your economy and service the global economy. Get the best brains from wherever you can, to help formulate such a strategy. Work out, for example, how, if a major investor comes into the country, the local small-business sector can profit. Make sure that this strategy is understood across government. To attract investment you need different departments to work together and to align. Set up the right process within government to make this happen.

As with the necessity of a strong macroeconomic policy, the need for good infrastructure may seem obvious. And, of course, all countries want the best infrastructure they can get. They know that without it their economy will be stunted. The problem—given finite resources and unlimited demand—is how they get it.

One of the reasons China has been able to achieve such

traction in Africa is that it has been willing to build infra-structure. The Leader wants a new bridge? A new airport? A new government building? The Chinese—government or private sector or state-owned enterprises (SOEs)—march in and get constructing. No political strings are attached. The problem is the other strings: concessions for resources or terms of debt, contracts negotiated at speed but later repented at leisure.

But it is this speed of delivery which has enabled China to expand trading links so rapidly across the develop-ing world. And it underscores the urgent demand for infrastructure.

It requires a plan, as ever. At its heart is a project which is investable. This is where things usually break down. "Investable" means in a form in which an international rep-utable investor can see the scope, the feasibility and, most vital, the rate of return. It can't just be a wish list of the presi-dent's favourite "blue sky" ideas.

The trouble is that making a project "investable" requires expertise that governments generally lack. This is why, for all the talk, the proportion of investment going to renewable energy in the developing world as opposed to the developed world has fallen in past years. It's not a shortage of capital. It's a shortage of projects put in investable form.

This offers a huge opportunity for the development pol-icies of the West if only some imagination were exercised in how to fill the lacuna.

My institute helps with this challenge in a lot of the coun-tries we work in, but governments for their part have to cooperate, and they also have to overcome the vested interests that benefit from the existing infrastructure arrangements.

Infrastructure, of course, serves both the country itself and its international trade. Take airport links, for example. The more connected and accessible a country is, the more investment is attracted. Direct flights from Europe and the USA, and increasingly from wealthier parts of Asia, are therefore crucial. So are procedures at the airport that minimise the hassle for the visitor. Ideally, there should be a national airline, though not necessarily one run by the state.

All of this is very challenging. With the right planning, however, challenges can be met. Singapore, the UAE and Qatar have drawn on government wealth to improve their connectivity. But then so have poorer nations such as Rwanda, which is building a successful airline, and Ethiopia, which has one of the best in the world.

Ports also need to be out of government hands—where they're often bastions of corruption—and world-class operators brought in. I know countries with masses of things to offer the world, where it can take weeks to get goods out of a port, unless of course money changes hands, which for Western companies today is simply impossible.

Power sector planning is essential, too, particularly in our technology-driven age. In developing countries, the management of national utilities is often inefficient, and, as a result, investors looking for a return can't see one. (As a rule developing nations will receive a certain amount from the international donor community for roads, and occasionally for railways and ports, while help with power generation is available but takes a lot of time and effort to access.)

The result is that some of the poorest countries have some of the highest prices for electricity, while big companies developing commodities use their own power supply disconnected from the national grid. In the work we do in this sector around the world, there is a game plan which can be followed to ensure investment flows and generating capacity is built. But it requires a strong focus from the Leader and the willingness to take on the interests holding back necessary reform.

One island state we work with has a warm climate and plenty of sun. There is therefore unlimited potential for cheap solar and wind power. What is it using? Expensive diesel. Nuts! Thankfully it's changing. But only because the Leader decided it was time to call out the local monopoly.

Today, digital technology is vital to infrastructure—so vital that I devote a separate chapter to it (Chapter 20). Here it should simply be noted that there is no part of a country's economic strategy that should go uninfluenced by technology.

Agriculture, for example, is about to undergo its own technological revolution: new methods of irrigation and fertilisation, new seeds, new forms of cooperative ownership achieved through digitisation, new ways of accessing markets, predicting weather, even indoor growing—but all developed through advances in technology which AI is about to boost enormously.

With a large part of the world still dependent on agriculture for employment, it is crucial for a Leader to study these developments and see how new methods can be applied.

There are countries—Sierra Leone with rice, Ethiopia with wheat—which have successfully engineered limited import substitution programmes. But the possibilities today offer the opportunity of an agri-revolution for countries prepared to engage with these new ways of working.

Amid all this, don't forget the labour market. Again, there are lessons to learn from developed and developing nations.

Some poorer countries have such informal economies that it really doesn't matter in practical terms what the letter of the law is in respect of labour rights, protection in the workplace and so on. But for middle-income countries looking to move into developed-country status, these are important. Middle-income countries are also often held back by old labour practices—restrictive usually—multiple vested interests and a web of different organisations that either make the business of employing people difficult or encourage the informal economy to continue. Again, for outside investors, such practices are a deterrent.

Take Indonesia. For years and through successive presidencies, it struggled with a system where, for example, there was a ban on using foreign doctors. The country's medical association had a tight grip on recruitment. The result was that the healthcare system was left severely short of personnel and the country spent a fortune sending people—at least, wealthier people—abroad for treatment, until, finally, President Jokowi produced an Omnibus Law of Labour reform, allowing at least some foreign doctors to practise to augment local ones.

Europe is an object lesson here for middle-income

countries. Our labour market laws, and pension schemes, were the product of highly centralised collective bargaining in the days of old-fashioned industry. Over time, and as the economy demanded more flexibility, these have become brakes on innovation and growth. Changing them is hard but essential. Because without a reasonable level of labour market flexibility, a country will struggle to obtain high levels of investment or growth.

This doesn't mean there shouldn't be proper protections in place—like a minimum wage, for example. But very restrictive practices around hiring and firing, while they may entail less firing, also mean less hiring.

Preparing people, educating them for a changing labour market is crucial, too. Universities today are not only centres of education, they're also business incubators. For Britain, which has some of the finest in the world, they're a vital part of UK PLC—representing a major shift in focus over the past thirty to forty years. The same is true of the USA. It's no coincidence that where there is a Stanford or a Berkeley or a UCLA, you find a plethora of successful technology companies; a similar pattern is found in Boston and, increasingly, in Texas.

The crème de la crème of students from developing countries will usually end up abroad. In the short term, this is inevitable. But even if this proves the case longer term, it is still necessary for such countries to have at least some well-functioning higher education institutions. Existing institutions seeking to upgrade themselves can sometimes benefit from a partnership with a well-established Western university. Most universities in Western countries have indeed established partnerships with those in a variety of developing countries—some of the partnerships have been facilitated by my institute.

It is worth developing countries' while to expend real effort to bring in such partners. They can accelerate development, and share expertise which then creates connections with international "best in class," in a way that a country could never achieve from a standing start.

Liberate your talented young people, particularly in the tech sector. In virtually every country in the world, there are smart young people switched on to technology who, if they're enabled, will invent applications, start small companies that can grow, disrupt traditional business models and do so with astonishing speed. I have seen this all over Africa and the Far East. There is amazing home-grown ingenuity. The role of government here is to create as much regulatory permission for such experimentation as possible, and to minimise bureaucratic interference or rules drawn up with an old-fashioned view of the economy in mind.

Some countries have built their own facilities for helping start-up companies, specially dedicated sites and offices where young entrepreneurs with interesting innovations can be helped to turn the ideas into businesses. These are called "incubators."

The result is that the smart young people who make use of those facilities have a chance to grow a business, employ people and create the ecosystem which can help the whole economy flourish.

Despite the frequent chaos of central administrations in many countries in Africa, and though the amount of venture

capital there lags behind the rest of the world by a significant degree, that capital has nevertheless increased tenfold
in the past five years. Africa is now home to around a dozen
impressive unicorn companies. The trend is even more
apparent in South East Asia.

It helps, too, if the country is a place people want to
come to. Security. Functioning cities. These matter. So, too,
do culture and art.

Finally, the government itself needs to be organised
to take advantage of opportunities to make these types of
economic change. Put your best people in charge. Bring
in whatever outside expertise you need. It is highly
unlikely that the existing bureaucracy will have the skill set
you require. But there will be outsiders—maybe in your
diaspora—who will sign up if called upon.

When the president of Indonesia wanted the best finance
minister he could find, he turned to Mrs. Sri Indrawati, then
at the World Bank. He asked her once. She said no. Twice,
she said no. Third time, like the parable in the Bible, his persistence paid off. Good people are gold. Go and find them
and ask until they say yes!

Economics always seems so very dry. But some of these
lessons if followed will change a country's trajectory. All are
difficult to put into practice, of course. But across the globe
you will find countries that have managed to do so.

I have left one element out. It is so important it needs its
own chapter: the rule of law.

CHAPTER FIFTEEN

The Rule of Law

When we consider the multiplicity of complex challenges that Leaders face, the grand and fascinating issues like the technological revolution, or how to cope with the rise of China, or the practical but essential lessons of winning or losing power, it may seem strangely prosaic to have a chapter on something that sounds as dry and niche as the "rule of law."

That, however, would be a grave underestimation of its importance. The rule of law is something every developed nation has in common. That alone should mean it gets some attention. Because it implies that it is intrinsic to becoming developed—and it is.

Consider the countries that have made it from "Third World" status to "Second World" through to developed nations; all of them—some with a lot of struggle—finally embraced the rule of law.

What is the rule of law? It is a legal system which is not corrupt, which operates according to objective principle, where experienced legal minds sift evidence, search for truth, and decide on the basis of what they judge, genuinely, to be right. In other words, a justice system that seeks to be just.

That doesn't mean it is flawless, or doesn't make

mistakes, occasionally miscarry justice; but it does mean it doesn't intend to.

Now, most people would agree it is morally correct to have such a system of justice. But the important thing to emphasise is the role it plays not just in the moral rectitude of governing but in its efficacy.

The characteristic people value most in any society is stability. It might not be the first thing someone in a modern developed nation thinks of. But that is because we take it for granted. The government loses an election, it goes. People break the law and we understand there are consequences. The system may underperform and let people down; but we know it's supposed to function properly and, if it doesn't, there will eventually be consequences. We can challenge government, express opinions, protest, stand for election in all manner of weird political groupings: essentially feel free, within accepted norms of behaviour, to do as we please.

Sure, people complain about "intrusive" government, and during Covid some even claimed we were living in a "police state" when we were told to vaccinate, but most of those people have no clue as to what living in a true police state is like.

Britain has been fortunate enough to possess the rule of law over a very long and unbroken period of time. There have been political upheavals, moments of acute national anxiety, wars, threats from terrorism and many crises, but throughout the foundational stability of the country has held firm.

The presence of the rule of law has been crucial to this happy state.

It would be hard to list all the people from abroad who say to me: we like your country because we know we can depend on your judicial system. One friend from a country where the judges routinely accept bribes told me of his pleasure and astonishment when he found that in the court case he litigated in London's commercial court—because he had wisely put UK dispute resolution in the contract—the judge seemed genuinely concerned with the facts!

Britain has made a good living from the law, as a matter of fact. Legal firms and the courts do well from the business of deciding cases fairly, because British, or more accurately English, common law is the law of choice governing the contracts.

The presence of a properly functioning legal system in any country makes the country inherently attractive. I know of international investors who say: I will only invest in a country that observes due process. You can tell them of the great opportunities in some developing nation, the potentially outsize returns they might make; but still they prefer the solidity and dependability of a country whose legal system means that they can get a fair trial if something goes wrong.

With faith in the law, people can plan, think ahead, be ambitious, be unrestrainedly creative. Without it, they reason: let me take what I can when and wherever I can, because who knows what tomorrow brings; and if I can only be creative in so far as I am allowed by an oppressive government, why should I bother in the first place?

Or you could be a good entrepreneur, have a great idea, believe that you can build a thriving business, but if that means upsetting the existing providers in the same line of business with the power to impede you, or getting permits from a bureaucracy which is subject to corruption, it means your full-time focus is on working the system, not scaling the enterprise, and spending your energies on circumventing the obstacles, not on the quality of the product.

In all this, a robust legal framework plays a significant part. You need to know that the existing providers can't take you down through their government contacts, that government officials aren't going to be asking for a pay-off, that there isn't some hidden hand thwarting you. And if there is, that you can challenge it.

Naturally, if you're some big global company, with its own power and contacts, you can go into almost any political environment and make deals, prosper and calculate the risks reasonably cleanly. Smaller investors or local entrepreneurs, however, suffer and are held back. And the impact is much bigger than you might think. In several of the developing countries in which the Tony Blair Institute works, sectors vital to the success of a modern economy are dominated by key traditional players, who keep out innovation by using their networks of contacts to stifle competition, and who maintain a (usually very cushy) status quo.

Energy and telecoms are two obvious areas. In the era of the technology revolution, they have much more centrality than ever before. Keep out innovation there and a country's potential is chronically constrained.

I know of countries with access to large amounts of natural resources for energy, who nonetheless rely on expensive fossil fuel imports, or whose power-providers can charge exorbitant prices because they have suppressed competition.

I know of countries whose need for satellite technology to bring internet connectivity to remote areas of the nation is abundantly plain, but who persist in blocking satellite providers because local telcos fear the competition.

For the economy, then, the rule of law is not a "nice to have," it is a critical element for future prosperity.

It's vital for political stability, too. Because if people know there is legal recourse, against discrimination or bad behaviour by officials, then they're more likely to seek change through persuasion than revolt. That doesn't mean there won't be demonstrations, marches and, if you're French, the occasional riot; but it does mean that the silent majority, whatever their view of the particular issue in contention, do not think "the street" is the way to decide the issue.

For developing countries who want to introduce the rule of law, the challenge is where to start. As with any other reform, whole-system change is hard and indigestible.

But there are ways to begin. Take commercial contracts, for example. Several countries have now ring-fenced contract law so that—if necessary, with judges from outside the country—companies investing can be sure of respect for contract law. It is vital for that to apply to local firms as well.

One of the many lessons in governance from the accession process to joining the European Union is the insistence, as part of passing the tests for adhesion, on the adoption of due process. Countries which were part of the old Soviet system of justice, which had become both politically and financially deeply corrupted, had to change their systems radically to comply. Now, it is true that some have treated compliance somewhat indifferently, but on the whole and certainly over time, there has been a huge change in those countries' legal systems, and for the better. The point is, it shows it can be done provided that the incentives to do so are large enough. And it does really matter.

I worry that, today, developed nations themselves, under the pressure of populist politics, are paying insufficient attention to the importance of the rule of law and its profound role in making our countries places where people want to be.

Judges should be able to do their work without interference from politicians—and especially without interference from the Leader—even when they're doing something the Leader—or for that matter, public opinion—dislikes. Change the legal framework within which they operate if you think that framework is seriously obstructing good government, but don't attack the courts when they simply interpret the law in ways you as Leader find inconvenient.

Media outrage shouldn't decide cases either. I'll read about a case in a newspaper and think "well, that's a weird judgment to make." But reading about it, especially if the paper is trying to make a point, is different from hearing it, listening to all the evidence and weighing that evidence to make a reasoned judgment.

And if a corrupted justice system is the most flagrant betrayal of the rule of law, an inefficient one damages it too. It's worth bearing in mind in this context the words of Magna Carta: "to no one will we sell, to no one will we deny

or *delay* right or justice" (my italics). Delay in legal processes in many developed countries, let alone developing
nations, undermines those countries and people's faith in
them. And the fact is that the legal systems of many nations
are in disarray. In the UK, for example, the criminal justice
system has pretty much broken down, with most crimes not
even resulting in a prosecution let alone a conviction, and
good cases collapsing because of the length of time it takes
to bring them to trial. I think the same could be said for
systems all over the Western world.

It doesn't help that the civil justice system is prohibitively
expensive for those on average incomes.

It doesn't help, either, that many systems were created
for a different time. The rules were set when people's primary
anxiety was a miscarriage of justice or police corruption or
malfeasance. The laws the systems are implementing are frequently out of date as types of crime—for example, online
fraud, drug-running, organised gangs—have changed in
nature and capability.

Technology is used randomly if at all, even though its
employment would enable massive efficiencies to be introduced in justice systems: in the preparation and conduct of
trials; in the writing of judgments; in taking evidence; and
even in civil cases in adjudication. Estonia is one nation
showing the way here, using AI to settle civil claims of under
7,000 euros and demonstrating, in the process, how AI
could play a significant part in helping developing countries
cut out low-level legal corruption.

We should also be wary of weaponising the justice system
politically. I choose my words carefully here. I am definitely

not saying politicians should be above the law. On the contrary. If a politician, especially a Leader, does something criminal, they should be treated no differently from anyone else.

But it is an increasing feature of democracies that Leaders come under criminal investigation, either in office or after, which takes place in a highly charged and politicised atmosphere. Sometimes the facts are in dispute. Sometimes the facts aren't but the characterisation of them is. And this is where the trouble starts.

OK, a Leader turns out to have a Swiss bank account into which government money has been siphoned off, or they have been paid by someone seeking to secure a government contract: of course, full force of the law.

But I don't like to see high-profile cases where the facts are open to different interpretations, where the case is borderline, and where, let us say, there is a certain transparent zeal with which the case is being prosecuted.

If even a small number of reasonable people think the system is being politically used, it undermines faith in the system. Worse, it allows someone who is genuinely criminal to mix up the justified with the unjustified and thus rally their support base in a manner poisonous to democracy. After all, if a Leader believes they're being targeted by the system in ways they think are naked politics dressed up in legal garb, they will fight to survive by attacking the system's integrity.

Then what is good for the government goose becomes good for the opposition gander when the government falls. As a result, over time, something essential to the rule of law, namely faith in the law's objectivity, becomes fatally weakened.

So, yes, apply the law to Leaders as to citizens, but there is no harm and much good in exercising judgement as to when doing so is truly necessary.

Anything that smacks of arbitrariness (and Western nations should take care in this regard with some of their actions on sanctioning individuals), or putting political power above legal process, or the diminution of objective in favour of subjective determination, should be avoided or permitted only in the most extreme of circumstances.

The rule of law is more than a set of rules fairly administered. It is a virtue, a quality which speaks to the nature of a nation. It is hallowed ground. Acquire it if you don't have it, to govern well; and if you're lucky enough to have it already, appreciate it and don't disturb it.

CHAPTER SIXTEEN

The Plague of Ideology

When I am in South America, I occasionally reflect that the worst thing Europe ever did to the continent—after colonisation—was the export of European political ideology, particularly some of the more fundamentalist types of socialism. Brazil, Argentina, Mexico, Colombia, Venezuela, not to mention the smaller countries, all bear the scars of the same ideological battles, and nearly all are still struggling to overcome them.

We could take some of the Middle East countries that were heavily influenced by European political thought and conclude the same: Nasser in Egypt or the Baath Party in Iraq or Syria.

This is not to say the military dictatorships also governing many of those countries were not as bad or worse; but that was less to do with ideology than a plain grabbing of power. And fascism as a functioning ideology in power thankfully died in the Second World War.

I am from the progressive wing of politics, the one that is traditionally associated with—among other things—socialism. And as a code of values, I still find socialism has great attraction. We should as a society look after the poorest first. We should as a community provide the services fundamental to human progress so that all the people, and not some, can benefit from them. Inequality of opportunity, and to a degree outcome, should be a scourge to our conscience. We should commit to those outside our borders as well as to those within them.

But socialism as a hardcore ideology—seeking to control the economy, regarding business with suspicion if not enmity, protecting the producer even at the expense of the consumer, believing that the bigger the state, the more just the country—has no appeal for me. This version of social-ism has done damage and continues to do it. And it is one of the ongoing tragedies of politics on the left that parts of the left carry on in adherence to this ideological view of socialism long after it has become clear that the chasm between the claims made for it, and the reality created by it, is unacceptably large.

In recent times, the Conservative wing of politics has developed its own ideological challenge.

Conservatives, traditionally, have had some good things going for them. They bring a perspective of realism to the process of governing. They're sceptical about utopian dreaming, because they understand it begins in excitement and ends in disappointment. They value hard work and self-improvement. While some on the left view patriotism and love of country contemptuously, Conservatives rightly regard them as positive qualities.

While I was growing up in politics, Conservatives dis-trusted ideology. They believed it incompatible with sound policy. They certainly stood for certain principles: free trade, social order, global engagement in defence of inter-ests and, latterly, equality of opportunity and aspiration.

They sometimes thought it necessary to take difficult or unpopular decisions to uphold these principles. True, there was something elitist about it all, but in a curiously healthy way. They thought that to govern well was an end in itself, and that bred with it a certain superiority complex. They thought that those on the left got misled into doing things which chimed with their ideology but not with objective reality. The Conservatives could be relied on to govern well because no one else would. Or at least that is how they saw things.

As a result, in Britain, the Conservative Party has been the default party of government, holding power for roughly three-quarters of the 120 years that the Labour Party has been in existence. (And even then, a third of Labour's time in office was under New Labour, about which the traditional Labour Party was somewhat conflicted.) In other words, because the Labour Party was often not a true competitor for power, the Conservative Party took the role of being a reliable if not always likeable guardian of the interests of the realm.

Then the Conservatives became intoxicated with the giddy elixir of ideology. How this happened, and why, we can debate. But suddenly, patriotism became nationalism, love of country became rejection of institutions of global cooperation, duty to govern well became the hallmark of the dreaded elites which they no longer wanted to join but rather to pull down around them.

This is not a phenomenon confined to Britain. Around the world we see traditional parties upended by new populist parties, or see mainstream parties increasingly captured by their fringe elements. There has been a hardening of politics around the left and the right.

The two ends of the spectrum have much in common. They both use the same inflammatory rhetoric. They both indulge in populism, which delights in exploiting grievances rather than dealing with them. They both demonise particular groups as standing in the way of the future they desire. For the left it could be business. For the right it could be immigrants. They thrive on confrontation and seek it out. They both find policymaking driven by evidence, analysis, deep thinking about difficult problems as proof of what a country is up against rather than necessary to provide solutions. Looking around the world and asking what works is seen as the refuge of the impure, the early signs of betrayal of "the cause."

The appeal is essentially to the public as victims—of the "deep state," the "blob," the media barons, the billionaires, the financiers, 57 varieties of the "enemy within." Complexity is an irritant. Facts are yours or mine; not just facts.

The rejection of ideology is not the same as rejecting ideals. I know that some would define ideology as something more akin to ideals, or at least a structured set of ideals. But for me the distinguishing feature of an ideology is that it is a whole-system analysis and solution. It is intrinsically dogmatic. For example, I would argue that the creation of public healthcare systems and welfare states was the product of ideals: they're compatible with different views about the economy, the market, the role of private capital; and they're motivated by values of human solidarity, not by doctrine. Ideology, on the other hand, is a belief system in which the state—or it could be a religion, or an idea—is not an answer but THE answer. It is a lens through which every challenge is seen and solved.

Ideals are more like principles—universal and non-exclusionary.

Anyone in politics should have some idealism in them. Even just a desire to run a country well counts as an ideal. Contrary to what most electorates think most of the time, the majority of people in politics go into it to try to do good. Naturally they don't always succeed. But that's another matter. Being motivated by principle, by strong values, a sense of purpose—these are great qualities. And necessary for the political game if it is to be played well.

Ideals are a live hand, measuring achievement by what is achieved. Ideology is a dead hand, measuring achievement by obedience to doctrine and dogma. Ideology is not even a governing political philosophy. It is unfortunately too rigid for that. It is a conviction that only a certain way or a certain set of policies or a certain set of fixed attitudes have validity and should prevail.

The appeal of ideology is that it promises to effect not just any change but "radical" change. And at a time of deep frustration with conventional systems and their outcomes, this appeal runs out of the fringes and into mainstream politics.

For the ideologue, being "radical" is paramount even if at odds with being "practical." People who are "practical" are considered at best technocratic, and at worst humdrum or even boring. No one ever captivated a street demonstration with a placard reading "Be practical."

But practical and radical should not be alternatives, in competition with each other. They should be complementary. Radical in the context of governing means fundamental change. Systemic change. Change that alters the rules of the game. But if it's not practical, it won't work.

Big problems require big solutions. But the emphasis should be on the word "solution" as much as on the word "big."

As I discuss later, harnessing the twenty-first-century technological revolution should be the goal of government today and one that is both radical in nature and practical in effect. In time, it will eclipse the twentieth-century ideological battle between state and market, capital and labour, and at least alter the background against which debates over globalism or nationalism are conducted.

When I think of the countries doing well today, they have done so by sound analysis, careful evaluation of the evidence, painstaking construction of policy and then have made change which is far-reaching based on what the evidence tells them will yield the desired consequence.

China's former leader Deng Xiaoping is a fascinating study on many levels. More than anyone else, he was responsible for opening his country up and creating the conditions for its extraordinary economic progress. He did so in the aftermath of the brutal ideological nightmare of the Cultural Revolution, in which a version of Maoist ideology gripped the country with disastrous effects. Deng himself was arrested, exiled, his family persecuted, yet somehow he re-emerged to lead what became increasingly a frontal assault on the very notion that ideology could or should distort an objective assessment of reality.

The words he used to persuade the Chinese Communist Party to change course so dramatically still resonate today.

Contrary to the CCP doctrine (and actually much of Chinese history), he asserted that China had to learn from others, in particular the West, from Western education to Western science and technology. He described the process of policy reformulation as "seeking truth from facts" and "proceeding from reality." To do that, he argued, people had to "emancipate" their minds.

Rather than vain boasts about how wonderful things were in China, he emphasised instead China's relative poverty and backwardness.

It was a remarkable and transformative message.

And he followed it up in what he called "integrating theory with practice," delivering fundamental reforms and changes to China's economy and system that set the country on a path to future prosperity and power.

His life, prior to being Leader, was a testament to the damage ideology can do. His leadership once he assumed power was a testament to what an enlightened Leader, free from the constraints of ideology, can achieve.

A Leader, even if they have come to office with support that is ideological in nature, would do well when in power to govern according to what works, what will produce change that is real, not fit the policy to the ideology but—even if quietly—discard the ideology in favour of the answer. The practical answer.

Stimulate and stir the emotions of the people of course—that is part of political leadership. But if you want to succeed, be that radical with the head and heart in healthy combination.

PART IV

Keeping Up with a Changing World: The Twenty-first-Century Technological Revolution

CHAPTER SEVENTEEN

The Technology Revolution and the Reimagined State

We are living through a twenty-first-century technological revolution that is transforming the way we work, live, interact with each other and engage with the world around us, and it is doing so in as powerful and all-encompassing a way as the nineteenth-century Industrial Revolution transformed the world of an earlier generation—possibly more so.

Yet it has not so far transformed politics. It should. And with it, it should bring about a reimagining of the state itself.

A few years back, when I first started making this claim to fellow politicians, some would nod, but most would put the statement down to typical political hyperbole. Or they would think I had been out of office for too long, that I was forgetting how "ordinary" people lived their lives, forgetting the cost of living crisis, the pressures of everyday existence—things that at one level, of course, seem a world away from computer chips and scientific discovery.

"It all sounds very technocratic," they would say. The word is not meant as a compliment in politics.

The sniffiness among political people towards anything which might be deemed "technocratic" or "technical" has always intrigued me. I first came across it when I was undertaking root and branch reform of the healthcare system in the UK, and colleagues—even those generally sympathetic—would say, "Yes, but what about the values of the British NHS, its fairness, its free-at-the-point-of-use clarity? Surely those are the key things?"

As if "values" and the technical means of achieving them were somehow in separate boxes!

The technical is the means of implementing the values. The better the technique the faster the progress.

Of course, the language in which the purpose of the reform is expressed should avoid technocratic terms, but without the technical part being correct, the reform will never succeed.

The word "technology" is a derivative of two Greek words: *techne*, meaning skill or craft, and *logos*, meaning word, and also thought (as in St. John's gospel—"In the beginning was the word"). The point is the word "technology" assumes there is a purpose to which the skill is being put.

Likewise, the word "technocratic" basically means people with specialist knowledge who can use that knowledge to solve practical problems; i.e., technocrats make things work.

This twenty-first-century technological revolution implies a fundamental change in the means to the end. Which is not to say the means is the end. The purpose of political activity and of government, done properly, has not changed. It was and is to advance the interests of the people and to implement the values underpinning that purpose.

But in this case, the nature of the change in "means" is so great that it enlarges the ambition of the end and the speed at which it can be attained. It is a revolution that offers the opportunity to solve problems to which there are presently no solutions.

The task of the Leader is first to accept the magnitude of this "real world" change, then to explain it, and finally to weave it into an exciting and enthusing political narrative.

The reality facing every developed nation is that the services the citizen expects can't keep up with the pace of demand. Healthcare systems are teetering on the brink; criminal justice systems are dysfunctional; planning consents slowing down or impeding essential changes in infrastructure, particularly in green energy; backlogs, breakdowns and bureaucracy abound.

The old answer was spend more, tax more.

But today, we're at the limit of public acceptance of tax and spend as the answer. Expectations haven't changed. The pressure for government to deliver is as great as ever. But the capability of doing so, with the state in its present form, has eroded.

The new answer lies in embracing fully the potential of technology to transform.

In the developing world, where the challenges are multiple, complicated and often seemingly intractable, and where finances are inevitably constrained, this technological revolution is the "leapfrog" idea, the thing which can allow a nation—and within a reasonably short space of time—to bypass the normal stages of development and accelerate rapidly to the future.

And it offers global solutions as well. There is no politically realistic answer to the challenge of climate change other than through the invention of technology which permits sustainable economic growth. Otherwise, in the developed world, consumers will rebel against the costs of action; and the developing world will put development action above climate action, because, after all, they didn't create the problem and they need their countries to grow.

So, the twenty-first-century technological revolution isn't AN issue, it is THE issue of our times. It should DOMINATE the political debate, not be an interesting sidebar to the "first order" daily living issues.

Twentieth-century political economy was dominated by debates around capitalism/the primacy of markets vs socialism/the size of the state—the traditional division between left and right.

For some years now, these debates have abated in significance even as they have intensified in fury. So, we argue about marginal changes to tax and spending and ascribe vast ideological difference to them.

Alongside them have come new "culture" debates—nationalism, "wokeness," identity—partly in replacement of traditional economic debates, where the extremes of positions overwhelm the public discourse, even though most people take a reasonable and more nuanced, moderate view of all of them.

Debating how we apply technology to solve our problems, in ways that don't threaten our liberties, is a less high-octane, emotionally thrilling ride than debating whether our opponents are good or bad people, but is ultimately far more fulfilling of our interests and happiness. However, it requires political Leaders to embrace this agenda and develop the narrative which provides the "thrill" and the enthusiasm.

Generative AI has, to a degree at least, changed the political mood around technology. Some Leaders will, for example, use ChatGPT. Even so, for most it remains a kind of toy. They don't yet think about how it can change entirely their political programme, as we shall see in the next chapter. Or they focus on the dangers of it, and talk obsessively of regulation—a conversation which comes naturally to the political class.

None of this is surprising. Back in the throes of the nineteenth-century Industrial Revolution, politics took ages to catch up with what was happening in the real world. Exciting new inventions were being made all the time; the development of urban centres and the reduction of countryside employment were proceeding apace. The economy of the UK as the epicentre of this revolution was being transformed.

But the political class, as a reading of the parliamentary debates of the time reveals, was still locked in the world of the previous age, dominated by wealthy Tory and Whig landowners. And much of the debate was around the "evils" of this industrialisation.

It took decades before such people realised that the new industrial world they were witnessing was THE issue and before legislation recognising its existence started to be passed.

It took even longer for the political party system to adjust to it. The UK may have been the furnace of the Industrial Revolution, but it was not until the early twentieth century that the British Labour Party was formed. It was not until the 1920s that it assumed power for the first time. It was even longer again before the British state itself was the object of the revolution and the modern welfare state was created.

In all, the process of change and adaptation took a hundred years.

Today's world moves much faster. But even so, it will take time for most to catch up. Eventually, political Leaders will begin to realise the enormous potential of such a new narrative and, in government, understand the capacity the technological revolution can bring to delivery and therefore to political success.

It will not necessarily be the countries we expect that start the process. Who would have thought that the government of Estonia would be the most technologically progressive in the European Union, or that Kenya would lead the way in smart processing of financial payments, or that Senegal would produce the best Covid-19 vaccination pass, or that Indonesia would come up with the most advanced mobile delivery service?

One key change this revolution will initiate is a fresh understanding of the centrality of education to economic achievement. In this new world, the university sector becomes a vital economic engine. No country hoping to succeed in the twenty-first century can be without world-class universities. Out of higher education will come innovation. And once a digital infrastructure is in place, local talent can invent new applications. A whole new eco-system of enterprise arises that can, if properly utilised, change both the local economy and government.

Traditional political parties formed along those traditional left/right economic fault lines will—indeed in many places have already started to—disintegrate and regroup around those conservative and hesitant about the application of technology vs those who see it as a future which should be embraced.

At this point people often go: "Stop! This revolution is terrifying!"

However, if there's another lesson to be learnt from the Industrial Revolution in particular, and history in general, it's that such things, once invented by human ingenuity, are never disinvented by human anxiety. The machine-breaking Luddites of the early nineteenth century tried to hold back the tide of change. They failed.

The answer, therefore, is not to resist or deny the revolution, but to understand it fully, to access its opportunities and mitigate its risks. Don't let fear or the inevitable campaigns against this revolution create hesitation. Let the sense of the opportunities energise the spirit of change.

Nothing makes me wish I was back in government more than the potential of this revolution. It's a great time to be governing.

CHAPTER EIGHTEEN

Hold the Press! Something Big and Breaking Is Going On

The unique scale of this technological revolution has one other attribute. It is evolving continually. And accelerating. So, what was impossible a month ago becomes possible. What seemed sci-fi is suddenly here and now. Today we're in the world of generative AI.

I say this as someone who understands the importance of the revolution, even if I don't fully understand the technology itself. And in using the word "fully" I am being generous to myself. There are huge gaps in my understanding of technology.

When asked some time back to give a speech at a cryptocurrency symposium, I first spoke with my son, who works in the tech sector, and asked for a briefing on the subject. He tried explaining it all to me. Complete incomprehension. He sent me something called "The Idiot's Guide to Crypto." Reading it proved that there is a stage of stupidity beyond idiocy, and that I appeared to have attained it.

Finally, on the morning, having read up what I could, I called him and went through what I had learnt up to that point. "What should I tell them, then?" I asked. "Tell them you're sick," he said.

But even though I don't understand fully how new technology does what it does, I know enough to know that what it does constitutes a revolution and not an incremental step.

The twenty-first-century technological revolution was already the game-changer for politics and had been for several years. But the very recent breakthroughs in artificial intelligence merit their own description as a revolution.

Just when you thought the pace of change could not get faster or more furious—with ever more complex geopolitics, Covid and its aftermath, accelerating climate change, wars in Europe and the Middle East—something is happening that is setting in train a further radical, technological transformation which will impact the real world massively, including all those geopolitical flashpoints.

Within an extraordinarily short space of time, certainly for the world of government and politics, generative AI will revolutionise our societies and economies.

I have always believed that there are essentially two sorts of brain: the emotional one which, if well developed, creates great art and culture and can, in politics, lead to success because it enables an understanding of the human factor in everything; and the scientific one, the one comfortable with maths and physics and chemistry, which can lead to great discoveries and game-changing scientific invention.

Quite early in life I worked out that, unfortunately, though desiring the second, I had instead been given the first. It's better than having neither, I suppose. But it has nonetheless been a continual source of disappointment to me. I was average at maths, poor at chemistry, and truly diabolically bad at physics—so bad that when I failed one particular exam my physics teacher told me with some awe that it was the worst paper he had ever encountered.

That awareness of my strength in one area and weakness in another is one of the many reasons I have always been against selecting children for overall academic prowess and splitting them between different schools accordingly—the old UK grammar/secondary system. The fact is that I was good at some things and utterly useless at others. I could grasp feelings—love, hate, respect, grief, anxiety, joy. I could see, touch and appreciate the physical world. But the world of concepts, of electrons, neurons, radio waves, gravity, conduction, electrical current—it all seemed like a closed book which I was virtually phobic about. I felt unable and, after a time, unwilling to prise it open.

Until recently, I didn't think that mattered, either for me or for the vast majority of politicians I know with "emotional" rather than "scientific" brains. I felt that it was good enough just to know what technology does. I don't know how a mobile phone works but I know how to use one. I don't know how a plane works—except very vaguely—but it doesn't stop me flying.

So why, with generative AI, do I feel the absolute necessity of understanding at least the basics of how and why this new breakthrough came about? Because I think that for a Leader to know even a bit about how it works will lead to a deeper realisation of why it matters so much. This, in turn, will bring clarity and, most importantly, urgency to the task of embracing the opportunities of this revolution and guarding against its dangers. Because both are HUGE.

So here, from the vantage point of an unscientific mind,

is what I think has happened. Needless to say, I write—ignoring the risks of gross oversimplification—as a Leader and not as a tech expert might express things.

Over the past decade, a series of technological break-throughs have created a reinforcement loop of self-sustaining momentum, a state of permanent technological revolution, in which different technologies merge and propel each other forward, resulting in a dramatic acceleration of innovation. These breakthroughs have their roots in inventions going back many decades. But they have finally come to an out-standing development in generative artificial intelligence which has profound implications.

We start with the computer, at first simply a machine capable of doing mathematical calculations via the data stored on things as simple as punch cards. Over time, that data became electronically stored. Originally computers were analogue—that is, they simply took signals (for example, sound waves) and mimicked them electronically, hence the name analogue (i.e., analogous). Then came digitisation—the capability to take analogue signals or data and encode them into digital signals, with everything broken down into two digits (0 and 1), according to the system of digital logic invented by George Boole in 1847. Signals transmitted by electrical current in this way have vastly enlarged capacity, are free from interference, and can be made more flexible. In other words, a digital circuit effect-ively involves a process which, manipulated or modulated, has far greater power than its analogue equivalent.

At first digital computers were vastly complicated electro-mechanical machines the size of a large room. But in the late

1940s and early 50s the first purely electronic circuits came along. Called transistors, they transfer the resistance necessary for the current to be regulated from one end of the device to the other. Transistors offer huge advantages over the bulky vacuum tubes that came before in that they are small and require relatively little power, and more of them can be stacked in a smaller space making for more effective transmission.

In 1959 came the first "integrated circuit": a number of transistors placed on one small strip of material, or "chip." The chip had to be made of a material that could transmit and regulate the current. This was the semiconductor material germanium soon displaced by the more efficient silicon.

With me so far?

It is no coincidence that many of those involved in the invention of the semiconductor chip worked at Bell Labs, the research offshoot of the Bell Telephone Company (named after the inventor of the telephone, Alexander Graham Bell), later the American Telegraph & Telephone Company. Telephones operated traditionally through wires connecting the power source to the instrument. But it wasn't long before researchers at Bell were experimenting with the use of electromagnetic fields and radio frequencies to transfer the power without wires. And integrated circuits or chips were the key to such experimentation.

At first, these wireless phones could be used only over restricted distances, serviced by a single transmitter tower, and they were very expensive. Then—once more thanks to inventions in Bell Labs—came first a network of wireless towers organised in what they called a "cellular" form; and, after that, a "switching system" that allowed a user to switch between different cells—hence the cellular network and, of course, the "cell" phone.

The first cell phone was launched in 1973 by Motorola's Martin Cooper. It marked the commercial coming together of two technologies: the transistor or semiconductor chip that allowed the phone to function without wires—to receive power, amplify the voice, connect to the frequency reliably— and the cellular phone.

The following years were a period of miniaturisation, as developers focused on ways to fit ever more data and processing power onto chips. In 1965 Gordon Moore, at that time director of research and development at Fairchild Semiconductor, predicted that the number of transistors capable of being placed on a chip would double every two years. Moore's Law, as it became known, turned out—unlike most political predictions—to be true. Today, it's possible to place billions of transistors on a single, small chip.

As smaller and more powerful transistors were being produced, another major breakthrough was made. At first computers could not connect with each other, or if they did, could do so on a very restricted basis—essentially, science lab talking to science lab.

But then a British scientist, Donald Davies, invented the concept of data blocks or "packets" being shared between computers. He did this through working out how to break data into discrete streams—packets—which could be transmitted between remote computers and then reassembled into the original form. This allowed computers to operate with much greater throughput of data and introduced a system of interconnected networks of computing, sharing such packets.

At the end of the 1980s, a British engineer, Tim Berners-Lee, working at the CERN facility in Switzerland, proposed a worldwide web, a system of universal linked networks inter-networking (hence the "internet"), accessible from any node on the network.

Other inventions proliferated: wave division multiplexing and fibre-optic cable radically increased the capacity of the system, allowing virtually instant communication and therefore email; mobile phones became connected to the internet, enabling an ever closer relationship between mobile and computer, as exemplified by the iPhone; Google invented its search engine, revolutionising browsing; the semiconductor chip gave rise to the Central Processing Unit, which effectively runs the memory system of the computer; and then the General Processing Unit (used in, among other things, video games), which allows the storing of images and videos.

Amid all this, the amount of data exploded: information, messages, social networks, images. It's extraordinary to think that 99 per cent of recorded human data has been gathered in the last decade. And it's thanks to this accumulation of data that analysis via algorithms—named after the Persian mathematician of the ninth century al-Khwarizmi—has become so powerful.

Algorithms are mathematical instructions that allow a step-by-step process of calculating and therefore analysing. The more data they have to call on, the better their performance. And as they grow in power, they can make ever better connections, spot patterns, reveal as well as record. They can predict what you might like, what you might buy, what interests you. Online shopping, Netflix and Disney, predictive text messaging, all work through algorithms.

They create a kind of rudimentary artificial intelligence.

And this is where the second modern technological revolution began. Until very recently, AI was just a very good conventional algorithm. You asked a question of the internet and it responded. The process was essentially reactive.

But the data kept growing. Moore's Law kept operating. Computers and mobiles were now completely interoperable. The things they could do kept proliferating.

Then came "cloud" computing. Once, everyone stored their data on their own servers. As the big tech companies grew—Microsoft, Amazon and others—they built such huge servers that they were left with vast amounts of unused space. They started to hire it out, using their data centres as places people could store their data without having to run their own servers with all the hassle of managing them, while simultaneously having access to much more computing power and better apps. Then other providers thought: hmm, there is a business in data centres. And so there was.

Don't ask why it's called "cloud" computing. There is a reason but frankly it's not worth the effort of explanation. And it's confusing. One political Leader I spoke to a couple of years back said, when I pressed on him the necessity of putting his government data on the cloud: "It wouldn't work here. The sun shines all year round."

For years scientists and technologists had tried to

replicate in artificial form the neural network of the human brain, the real AI. They hadn't got very far. Indeed, after a splurge of activity and funding in the latter part of the twentieth century, AI rather went out of fashion.

But then the explosion of data, and the vastly improved algorithms to analyse it, led to a resurgence of interest. The twenty-first-century AI equivalents of the Bell Labs pioneers of the twentieth century built new algorithms designed like the neural networks of the human brain and used them on what are called large language models (LLMs)—models that are huge (large) software systems, run on massive computing power, that can be trained to hoover up all the words (language) on the internet and, through AI, process them, detect patterns, make connections, answer questions asked of them, and give the appearance of thinking like a human.

Finally, like a child—which as a baby can't speak but is learning all the time the patterns of sound which eventually will lead it to speak—something changed. The machine moved beyond baby AI. And in 2022 the breakthrough occurred.

The machine could TALK!

It could propose. And therefore not just predict or describe but generate. Or, at least, it could do something close to a human mental process (though, of course, also open to "hallucinations").

What this means for us now is not just that processes can be automated with increasing accuracy and scope, but that AI can suggest new ways of performing them. At a certain point with Moore's Law, transistor miniaturisation reaches a physical limit. But with AI, a new chip can be invented that makes better use of existing transistor capacity, and so bypasses the limitations of Moore's Law. So, we now have the first AI supercomputer chip.

What does that do? It makes LLMs even better, able to do even more, creating in their wake even more data, which enables even better LLMs. In other words, it helps create a reinforcement loop of permanent revolution in innovation. Analogous to Moore's Law, this new AI—which we call generative AI because it has the ability to generate original content and thought—will exponentially increase in capability at a self-sustaining rate.

It has all human experience. It has human brain-like capabilities—BUT one with an ever-improving intellect. It can mimic both human experience and the human brain.

True, at present, it resembles a person with an average IQ of around 100—though a person who has also absorbed the experience of all 300,000 years or so of human existence. But as the reinforcement loop gathers momentum AI will soon have an IQ of 150—that's very smart. In time, it will have one of 200. And then we're in a new world.

Less remarked upon is the impact generative AI is having and will have on robotics. This could well usher in its own revolution, as if we weren't busy enough! Self-driving cars and drones are a reality already. Robots are performing essential manufacturing jobs now. There are even some taking orders in restaurants. But as the LLMs grow in power and sophistication, so the robots will grow in capacity and function. If there will be little limit on what GenAI can tell you or work out for you, so the robots will be able to perform complicated tasks—and as well as or better than humans.

Imagine robots that can cook, do your shopping, clean the house, plan your day or holiday, mow the lawn, even be a carer. They can perform elements of these tasks already. But imagine much more developed systems, which can not only respond to human instructions, but improve them, make them more effective, suggest as well as obey. The advent of the humanoid robot is here—still at an early stage, but over time, possibly a short time, this technology will accelerate. There are even those working on how we replicate human biology, so a humanoid robot really does resemble an actual human.

Think of a world in which robots can make up workplace and skill shortages, transforming productivity, indeed eliminating it as a challenge.

Before anyone points out the obvious, let me acknowledge it. Yes, there are mind-boggling risks in all this. AI is general purpose technology. It can be used for ill as well as good. It will require regulation of a revolutionary and deep nature. The fact remains, though, that just as the technological revolution I described in the previous chapter cannot be disinvented, neither can generative AI.

There is always with something so new a risk of hype and overstatement. But I think the better judgement is that it isn't another step on the same path, even a large one. It's a revolution all in and of itself. It will change everything. The future will now be different.

We don't know exactly what form AI will now take. Or what its next iterations will do. But we do know that it is life-altering. It won't necessarily replace all human activity. It may be more like a really able co-worker. But it will certainly affect every human task, every business. Every process the human brain can perform, AI will be able to do, faster and better. It will make possible major developments in science and technology in every field from medicine to fighting climate change. And, yes, it will give bad actors, already using cyber attacks to cause enormous harm, access to weapons of far greater potency and deadliness.

At an individual level, it means we all have to go back to school. And that includes Leaders.

At government level, it means not just a step change in understanding, but a preparedness to master and harness what AI can do.

Get that and you can succeed. Ignore it or underestimate it and you will fail.

CHAPTER NINETEEN

Applying Tech: A Reimagined State in Action

OK, so we're all agreed: we're in a new world. There are amazing opportunities. There are also frightening risks. How, then, do you make the most of the first and mitigate the second?

A Leader should begin by accepting one reality. Unless you're the president of the USA or China or possibly the Leader of a country with expertise in AI like the UK, or a body with weight like the EU, or "on the way up" like India, your ability to affect how computer technology in general, and AI technology in particular, develops, is somewhere between limited and non-existent.

So, there is literally no point in agonising over whether this twenty-first-century technological revolution is good or bad; whether and to what extent regulation is needed (though it definitely is); or whether it is right that the huge tech companies have the power they do. By all means take part in international conferences and conversations to discuss views on all this, and how best to manage things. But accept that, ultimately, you are not going to decide the contours of this technological revolution. However, you do get to decide whether you make the most of it.

Focus your leadership on that. Because the fact is, just as those nations that took their cue from Britain and industrialised nations in the nineteenth century thereby revolutionised their prospects, so those countries that fully harness new technology—and particularly AI—will undergo huge transformation. Think Japan in the late nineteenth century, which embraced the Industrial Revolution. Compare it with China, which didn't.

The crucial point about these revolutions—nineteenth-century industrial, twenty-first-century technological—is that we call them revolutions because after a revolution nothing remains the same. It may, at times, be incrementally implemented, but it is not, in the end, an adjustment of a system but a radical alteration of the basic principles underpinning it.

This is what you as a Leader should recognise. And adapt your mindset accordingly.

There are many things that affect a nation which are outside its control: the state of the world economy, disruption of supplies because of regional conflict, rising dollar or oil prices. All these have a direct impact on the living standards of a country's citizens. The best a Leader can do is to mitigate the impact, not remove it.

The technology revolution, by contrast, offers the chance to do things that have a real impact in a reasonably short space of time—within an election cycle—and that are within a government's control, at least if they can get the right partners to assist.

Imagine something utterly simple and prosaic: choosing a restaurant to eat in. Suppose every meal you had ever eaten, your opinion of each, the interplay between quality and cost, and the complete, not partial, knowledge of every restaurant now available to you within a defined radius, could all be assembled and analysed, you would for sure get a better answer to that choice than by trying to remember all that information, plus googling the local fare. And quickly too.

Now transfer that process to something much more significant: a surgeon performing an operation and calling not only on his or her own experience and knowledge, but the accumulated knowledge of all those who had ever performed the same operation. The outcome would be much better, wouldn't it? And then suppose that a machine—a robot—created through the same processes could do some of the trickier parts of that operation for the surgeon. That would be better, too, surely?

Think of clinical research and drug development, which generally takes years and costs vast sums, but which, thanks to new technologies, could be successfully trialled and brought to market at almost infinitely greater scale and speed, with goal shots multiplied a hundredfold. The pharmaceutical industry would, of course, be disrupted but in a wholly beneficial way.

AI is the only realistic answer to improve productivity in the private sector.

It will also create the possibility of transformative public sector change—reform on a scale never contemplatable before. It will allow the reimagining not just of the way a service is organised but of its essential purpose.

In Britain, at present, the purpose of the National Health Service is to cure the sick. But is that function actually the correct one? Properly thought through, the aim of any healthcare system should not be to cure the sick so much as to help people live healthy lives for as long as possible. Yes, that includes curing them if they do fall sick. But a health service's fundamental purpose should be to stop them becoming ill in the first place.

What is involved in fulfilling that purpose? It's things like identifying at birth or even pre-birth an individual's predisposition to certain diseases and conditions; making sure that young people are taught how to live healthily and are informed about the importance of diet and sport; ensuring that nutritional food is easily available and unhealthy food is not; sequencing everyone's genome; introducing regular health checks, either by the doctor or, increasingly, by the individual, and the data reported to the medics; giving people easy access to their own medical records so that they can share them as necessary; using data to improve procurement and develop new drugs and treatments at speed. And this is just for starters.

At present most education systems are there to get students through exams. But is that purpose the correct one? Exams certainly have their place: passing them involves commitment and discipline—both important qualities. But surely the true goal of education should be to equip students for life, so that they can get the job they want, know how to live well and be happy, well-adjusted people? If that is acknowledged, then—bearing in mind everyone is different—the current educational cookie-cutter approach is the wrong one. We need to take advantage of technology to enable pupils to learn at different speeds, absorb the knowledge that most suits their individual interests and abilities, and, above all, to think creatively in a fast-changing world.

Think of creating an AI doctor, which can assist a physical doctor, or which can help a person access the highest quality medical advice instantaneously; or an AI nurse working alongside a real one.

Or an AI tutor, which anyone at any stage of learning can use as a personal teacher on any subject. And do so interactively, as if talking to a real teacher who happens to have all the knowledge of humanity at their disposal.

Take the criminal justice system. Its purpose should not be the narrow one of punishing criminals but the broader one of keeping us safe. Of course, punishing criminals forms part of that purpose (and it should be done effectively and promptly, which by and large it isn't today) but it shouldn't define the whole of it. Once we focus on a system that will keep us safe we engage properly with schemes to design out crimes like online fraud, to deter violence and street crime, to make sure we use data, DNA; modern techniques of surveillance and scheduling to make policing effective, to make courts functional and show citizens that they're well protected and that, if that protection fails, they will have proper redress.

My institute keeps a running list of practical applications of new technology by governments across the globe; and it is growing all the time. Here are a few examples from developing nations:

- Drones and sensors are being used to map agricultural production, predict weather and check if stocks of grain and fertiliser provided by government are being properly utilised.

- The same tech is being applied to a deep analysis of mineral deposits, allowing many countries for the first time to assess the true nature and extent of the natural resources they possess.
- Tech is being brought to bear on water irrigation and seed enhancement to improve yield and transform the current situation whereby often an African nation will lag four- to fivefold behind what other developing (let alone developed) countries do.
- Telemedicine is making medical consultations and care possible in remote areas where a full medical presence is not practical, and generative AI will help put the doctor's notes in the right form and suggest treatments.
- Off-grid and mini-grid electricity is bringing power to remote or sparsely populated outlying regions and islands and, combined with satellite technology, is also giving them transformative internet connectivity.
- Cheap mobiles and tablets are being developed for those in the poorest parts of the world who find smartphones too expensive.
- Extensive tech facilities are being developed in Africa to help translate some of Africa's 2,000 local languages and so enable better communications.
- Welfare and subsidy payments are being made directly to the citizen or farmer, cutting down the risk of corruption.

- Personalised tutoring is now a realistic possibility open to everyone, thanks to companies like CK-12 Foundation and Khan Academy, a not-for-profit organisation that provides lessons online to millions, so using technology to bring top-quality teaching to under-served schools.
- Borders are being tracked to help eradicate smuggling, make sure fuel and tobacco taxes are paid, and eliminate "ghost" employees from the public sector payroll.
- A new range of vaccines and injectables is being developed for such communicable diseases as TB and HIV/AIDS and non-communicable diseases like heart conditions and cancer. With the right digital infrastructure in place, and proper health records— things which are freely available now—the health of a nation can be radically improved.

But most of these innovations happened before generative AI was fully developed. All of them and many more new inventions and innovations will be available through generative AI and probably on a scale we can, as yet, barely imagine.

The toughest thing for Leaders regarding this all-encompassing revolution is getting their heads around the enormity of the possibilities. It *is* a revolution. It *is* a fact. And it's up to each Leader to decide what use to make of it. And in a political environment fraught with problems and a seeming impotence to make conventional policy change, it offers a one-off opportunity to move the needle, and in a way that is not marginal but mould-breaking.

169

Not everything will happen at once. But over time, the nature of the state—what it does, how it does it, its relationship with its citizens—will change. Best practices from around the world will be available to copy.

It is truly exciting, but it won't happen without Leaders who have the self-discipline to get an understanding of this revolution and have the courage to make the changes consequent upon it.

But if they do, the rewards will be great for the nation and the Leader.

CHAPTER TWENTY

Building the Infrastructure

A reimagined state means a new creation, not just a revamping of the old state.

Think of it like your country starting an airline. You supply the airport, the logistics, the roads to and from the airport; the passenger services; and related industries in tourism and business.

But you would never dream of trying to build the planes yourself. Instead, you would buy them from Boeing or Airbus, or maybe Embraer or one of the other smaller but still large manufacturers. After all, those plane manufacturers have invested countless billions, have long experience, have teams of highly skilled operatives. In other words, they have attained a level of expertise, competence and safety that no country starting from scratch is going to be able to match.

It is the same with the digital infrastructure for a nation. Countries need to harness the technological revolution effectively, with, for example, national data management systems, where the entire data of the country is stored securely and is available for analysis. But to do so they need to partner with an expert in the field, which might be one of the smaller players around, but is most likely to be one of the giants: Amazon, Microsoft, Google or Oracle; and, in

China, Alibaba or Tencent. The choice of partner must be made carefully; and, of course, countries may decide—and probably, if large, should decide—to have more than one.

There is a justifiable anxiety about the domination of this market by big companies, as indeed is the case with mobile devices like smartphones. It is always possible that new players or new technologies will emerge, which make this domination redundant. But their size is worth dwelling on for a moment.

Apple has a market capitalisation as large as the annual GDP of France. Amazon in 2024 will spend four times as much on research and development as the entire R&D budget of the British government. Oracle has invested billions in making its cloud system secure. Microsoft invested $10 billion, a sum larger than the R&D budget of any European country apart from Germany's, in ChatGPT, the generative AI company. And that despite the fact they had absolutely no guarantee it would work. When Google bought DeepMind, the UK AI company and a world leader in the field, they then poured billions of dollars into helping it grow. No UK government could ever have diverted that level of investment into the company, vital though it is for Britain's future.

Now, you may dispute that it's good that these companies have such levels of cash to spend. You may feel there should be better ways to hold their extraordinary power to account. But the fact remains that they're able to make investments that ensure their products are vastly superior to anything anyone else can produce.

Generative AI has now added yet another dimension to

the infrastructure. The foundation models for generative AI—the large language models—will also be likely dominated by another handful of companies: OpenAI, Elon Musk's Grok, Gemini from Google, Meta's offering, though there are some smaller companies, like the French company Mistral, rapidly expanding with funding readily available. But again, the investment into these companies has been massive.

The computer capacity necessary to run these LLMs is vast, beyond the reach of most countries. So there will be a case for forming a partnership with one or more of the providers, to access the technology, though even then a country will have to provide the electricity necessary to power the model.

A country should be able to add its own data to the foundational model and create a bespoke LLM, by which the opportunities to innovate and improve efficiency on the back of it will be enhanced.

The investment for a country to build its own foundational LLM will be huge, though some like the UAE are doing so. But the cost of adapting an existing model and adding a country's own proprietary data is much less. I expect most countries and most large companies—also with their own data—will undertake such adaptations.

Digital ID will become an essential part of this digital infrastructure. Governments from Singapore and the Gulf States to India and Eastern Europe are using digital ID to transform the relationship between individuals and the state— a single biometric identifier that enables each citizen to access government services directly. At a stroke, bureaucracy—and therefore, in many countries, corruption—is cut out. Digital ID can allow people to access private sector services as well, paying for them directly and digitally.

Digital ID raises not only the challenge of changing existing legacy systems, but also the need to address people's fears about confidentiality and potential invasion of privacy.

To my mind such fears are generally misguided. Your average person gives more information to Facebook, TikTok, online shopping and entertainment than they would ever need to give government. And where, in an autocratic system, the government might abuse data privacy, frankly they're likely to do that anyway.

However, any sensible government will want to put systems in place which have proper oversight of digitisation, which enshrine citizen protections in law, and which give redress in the case of breaches.

Countries will want to protect data sovereignty. Leaders should interrogate the best way to do this. There is a common misconception that their data is safe, provided they host it in country. Unfortunately, that is incorrect. In some countries the electrical supply is insufficiently reliable, so backup systems are required. Cloud systems should be more secure, particularly if combined with in-country data centres.

Before embarking on a plan for the digital infrastructure, a Leader would be well advised to undertake a proper analysis of what digital capability already exists—and by "proper," I don't mean one undertaken by the system.

The system may well tell you that it's in control of the situation, that it's building the infrastructure and systems required, that the Information and Communication

Technology (ICT) Ministry knows what it's doing. It may sincerely believe this, by the way, but it will invariably turn out to be bull. On closer inspection you will discover that the infrastructure and systems are inadequate, the ICT Ministry is hopelessly underskilled, a myriad of local interests are getting in the way, and that any data centres you were hoping for are either poorly operated in the cloud or not there at all.

This is where the choice of partner really matters.

And where you're partnering with one of the big companies, demand, as part of the deal, that the company you choose comes with a skills and training offer, and use that to build a proper academy of digital education.

And send the word out to the tech world—this time not the big companies but the technological innovation community large and small—that your country has the right digital infrastructure in place and is open to companies coming with their product and experimenting with its application using that infrastructure.

Make your country a "sandbox" where—under supervision, of course—new innovations can be trialled. The sheer scale of invention out there is remarkable, but very often the inventors have no idea of the broad world outside the limited markets of the USA and Europe, and are constrained by bureaucracy and regulation there. They are frequently of an idealistic frame of mind, which would leap at the chance to help the developing world. If they knew how. You need a regulatory environment that encourages and facilitates technology solutions and draws in innovation from around the world.

Above all, understand that the better your infrastructure, the more opportunities there will be for local businesses to thrive. With the right regulatory environment and digital platform, you will quickly find a plethora of local talent emerging that will provide a broad range of apps, locally invented. Jobs will flow. And service transformation will be possible.

All this will require big changes in the skill set and mindset of government itself. A century of slow evolution in the process of government—its structures, skill sets, means of governing and accountability—needs to be disrupted.

So, it is one thing to understand in theory that this twenty-first-century technological revolution should change everything. It is another to build the capability to exploit its potential. And it is another again to use that capability to greatest effect in changing public services and the economy, so the reimagined state becomes a reality.

CHAPTER TWENTY-ONE

Derangement, Not Rearrangement: What Government Can Learn from Tech

The French word *déranger* has always amused me. In French it has the meaning of "disturb" as in "would it disturb you if I switched on the TV?" In English it has the much more alarming meaning of "deranged," i.e., mad, mentally disturbed, of unsound mind. "Would it derange you if I turned on the TV?" Hopefully not.

The derivation is from the French word *rang* or Old French *ranc*, meaning row, as in rows of soldiers or objects in order. It is where we get one meaning of the word "rank" from. *De-rang* means, as you would expect, changing the ranks, i.e., disordering what had been arranged in orderly fashion.

Government systems have their own very precise arrangements. They operate in traditional ways, with fixed methods, according to precepts of long-standing duration. Policy is usually built around certain "givens"—practices or principles which have grown up over the years and which circumscribe the boundaries of policy in any area; and how necessary it is to be willing to rethink them.

I didn't reflect much on this when in office, and to be fair the technology revolution was only just getting under way. As in so many other areas, since leaving office I have had the opportunity to enlarge my knowledge and analyse not just the impact of technological innovation, but the mode of thought applied by those innovating. I have found it fascinating and instructive.

And, obviously, I have wondered whether the same mode could be applied to government. I think it can be, or at least it is worth understanding how that mode works and how it might be.

Essentially, my conclusion is that the tech innovators are engineers, not just because that is sometimes literally their discipline, but because the word accurately describes how they approach a problem.

What I mean by this is that they look at an issue completely *de novo*. They abandon all preconception. They examine it end to end, working out whether the way it's done now is the way it needs to be done.

They realise you can't fix it without touching it, i.e., sticking your hands right into it, dissecting, disaggregating, "disturbing" the assumed natural or established order of things.

Often in business and certainly in government, people are asked to change things without touching them. "Yes, we want the system to work better; reform it but you can't touch the fundamentals because they're the established order." Result? Nothing changes. Because, of course, if the system itself was working, the question wouldn't be asked.

A business flounders when the world around it is changing and—probably—some technological innovation is rendering the business model obsolete. The only business strategy which works is one that recognises the necessity of rethinking the model. Very painful; but without it, the enterprise is doomed.

This is the right approach for an existing business faced with the challenge of change. And the same is true of a business started with the purpose of disruption. Both require a "from the beginning" examination leading to insight.

Virtually every major oil and gas company in the world is rethinking their future, trying to turn from being oil and gas companies to being energy companies. If they don't, they risk obsolescence, not short term but longer term, as the imperatives of climate change and the additional competitiveness, over time, of clean forms of energy take over.

And there is a reason why the top ten companies in the world were barely in existence twenty-five years ago. Technology has disturbed traditional business.

Tesla is now the largest car company in the world by market cap. Except it isn't really a "car" company. It is also one of the world's largest makers of batteries. It has built one of the largest factories in the world, the newest and most effective robots; redesigned the material to make cars, the way the materials are made, the electronics inside the car. It has one of America's largest data centres. (In a similar way BYD—the Chinese electric vehicle company—started life as an energy generation and storage company before going on to become an industrial giant.)

SpaceX has made the most effective rockets, better than those built by NASA, or China or Russia or anyone else.

Today, in Africa, if we want rural connectivity to the

remote areas of a country, satellite not cable will be the way to achieve it, faster and at much lower cost. Starlink has put more satellites into space than the rest of the world combined.

All of this has happened through the ingenuity of teams assembled by one extraordinary innovator—Elon Musk.

What is interesting to me is the way he has re-engineered every step of production. Yes, the car will be electric. But it needs a battery. The right ones for the car don't exist, so create them. Eventually it will be self-driving. So it needs hyper-complex electronics powered by AI. The metal should be lighter but more resistant to crash damage. Make it by robots for efficiency and speed. But there aren't ones available. So invent them. Why have a vast network of salesrooms? Just let the customer order the car online and have the capacity to ship immediately.

Why send space rockets into space which can't be reused? Work out why that is the case and change it.

Make satellites smaller, cheaper and easier to launch, and then launch thousands.

The point is both in the literal and figurative sense: there is in train a vast process of re-engineering.

Advances in AI—especially generative AI—computing power, clean energy like hydrogen and fusion, and big steps forward in bioscience—all create possibilities of change and the disturbing of the conventional ways of working, unimaginable a few years back.

Of course, it is one thing to understand these changes. It's quite another to apply them effectively, unless you adopt an engineering mindset.

Recently I have become acquainted with a company reimagining agriculture—specifically indoor growing. It was the brainchild of Larry Ellison, with whom my institute has a partnership, and who is the founder of Oracle, the data giant. The idea is to grow food close to the point of consumption, of higher quality and nutritional value than that currently available and with a continual not seasonal cycle of production.

Of course, greenhouse growing has a long history and a traditional way of being done. And so when Larry and his team came to consider how to build the new company they began with a limited number of useful innovations in seeds and cultivation, while utilising a conventional glass and metal greenhouse.

But over time, they realised that, to maximise the benefits of indoor growing, which began as a simple way to avoid the vagaries of the local climate, they had to reinvent every step of the process, from bioscience to make the best seeds, to robotics to pick the fruit, to new ways of managing heat and light, to a wholly new material for the construction of the greenhouse. Each step along the way was reimagined, if necessary, a new system of production created, while—here is what is interesting—using as much engineering expertise as agricultural know-how. Bringing in people from outside the area of agriculture allowed the development of completely new thinking because they were not bound by any conventions, but could look at the problem through an entirely different lens.

Now let us try to apply the same reasoning to government, to the state.

As I pointed out earlier, services like health or education

or criminal justice can be changed to serve a deeper purpose: moving healthcare from cure to prevention of illness; education as a means of personal improvement through life; criminal justice as making us safer not only punishing crime.

But think about the state itself and how AI could transform it. Government is all about process and AI should be able to automate large chunks of it.

It should need far fewer people working for it in traditional public service "process" jobs. And different types of people: often domain experts who can apply technology effectively, alongside more traditional guardians of the public interest—civil servants. But these civil servants would be relieved of a lot of the tedium of government bureaucracy and therefore be better able to give advice and prevent problems with a much better chance of being right.

The state would be more strategic: setting frameworks of regulation but doing much less implementation.

Systems of accountability would be much more accurate and much simpler, because the data would yield much better evidence of what was working and what wasn't.

The state would do much less controlling and much more empowering—it could make individual choice easier to exercise. It wouldn't be less powerful when it needed to have power to stop bad things, but it would have much less power to interfere unnecessarily because the bureaucracy would be much less.

For this to be done, there needs to be a recognition that re-engineering the state requires a different approach to governance; not just a reform but a reimagining.

Embarking on such a serious and deep reshaping of the

state is a huge political mission. It requires careful study and analysis, a coherent plan, a willingness to push forward and accept that there will be errors and missteps along the way, and an explanation as to why it should happen and the benefits of it. In the end, though, it should ensure better outcomes at reduced cost and therefore allow lower taxes or higher expenditure on things which at present are underfunded.

Everything else is secondary to this. Otherwise, we are locked in a fruitless and ultimately dispiriting debate about how we extract more from the same system with tweaks, and in a twentieth-century political fight over margins of tax and spending, which do nothing to alter the fundamentals of how we either tax or spend.

So, if we want derangement and not rearrangement, we need to think like innovators and not guardians of the system.

PART V

Foreign Policy

CHAPTER TWENTY-TWO

International Affairs: The Importance of Being Consistent

A funny thing happens on the way into government. Before government rarely does foreign policy feature that much in a Leader's mind. It may do if there is some big all-encompassing event, with domestic political implications. But otherwise it is the daily-bread issues which predominate— living standards, health, education, crime, immigration and so on.

But once in government—and reasonably fast—foreign policy does loom large.

And here, as in everything else, strategy is key. In fact, particularly so. Foreign policy requires definition. Don't stumble about in a series of disjointed manoeuvres. Think deeply about where your country fits in the geopolitical landscape under your leadership and why.

Unless your country is a major power, you will have limited influence in controlling its status within the global order. But you do nevertheless need to know what its place is. By this, I mean you need clarity on where it stands, who it stands with, how it wants to be regarded internationally. Your allies (and sometimes your enemies) need to know what your position is.

How does a country balance—in a changing and now multi-polar world—the different attractions, vulnerabilities and necessities of relationships West and East? How does it form or sustain the right alliances to protect its interests?

International relations will involve tough choices, albeit in a different way from domestic policy. But a lot of the time foreign policy is relatively easy, waters are smooth, the sailing is plain; captaining the Ship of State can be quite relaxing, even enjoyable, without the destabilising squalls of the political weather back home.

But come a big global moment, a veritable geopolitical tsunami, or even a mere storm, the captain better get on deck and choose which way to steer. At that point the compass you have, as Leader, carefully constructed, if indeed you have done so, becomes essential. And if you haven't, the damage can be quite substantial.

A friend to everyone and an enemy to no one is a principle most countries would like to follow. But it never turns out like that. A crisis arises and there are different sides. For example, Russia and Ukraine. Two sides—with their respective allies. Those nations which have tried to avoid picking a side have ended up pleasing neither, unless, as the Gulf States have done, they have been able to offer something—in their case economic—to give both parties an interest in keeping their relationship with them strong.

Unless your country is uniquely placed in some way, the risk of trying to please everyone is that—rather as in domestic politics—you end up pleasing no one.

As British prime minister I had a very straightforward

framework for foreign policy: America's closest ally; strong partner to Europe; and in the new Department for International Development, a top-quality soft-power asset deployable in the developing world. Each of these positions was clear, and the relationships pursued complemented and compounded each other.

So, at one level, there was definition and it worked.

Maintaining the relationships, however, could hurt politically.

Post-9/11, I decided we would be "shoulder to shoulder" with the USA. Easy to say. But then through the campaigns in Afghanistan and Iraq, the UK had to decide whether to be a real ally, making real commitment, or whether it would merely cheer from the sidelines. We chose the former and there will be many who think that choice was wrong. But I believed it was crucial for Britain in the long term to remain America's closest ally, because it would serve our deep interests.

The point is, for these purposes, not to debate which choice was right but to underline both that it *was* a choice and that such foreign policy choices can be really tough. Only the foreign policy experts sitting in their armchairs believe in the "have your cake and eat it" philosophy of policymaking.

Relations with Europe were never plain sailing for me either. Britain, as we know, is Eurosceptic. Ever since Margaret Thatcher took her handbag to a European Council meeting to demand a fairer deal on European finance for Britain, an exceptional case where Britain was rightly correcting an injustice, banging the table became for a large part of British opinion the gold standard for how you routinely conduct European business.

I would be attacked after every European Council meeting for not sticking it to my fellow Leaders in the name of "standing up for Britain." Of course, in a myriad of ways when promoting British interests, I would need those Leaders' trust and support, so it would have been an immensely foolish way of behaving. But had I gone with the political flow, life would have been a lot easier.

Even with development, my government's insistence on increasing the aid budget and being a leading player in the developing world, which again I thought essential for the country's long-term interests, was politically highly controversial. Had we put it to a referendum we would have lost that one too!

Where a country stands, who it stands with, what the guiding principles are and what price you are prepared to pay for upholding them, these are integral to the foreign policy strategic thinking a Leader must do.

There are big power relationships, which most often will require countries to search for actions they can take to protect those relationships and give the big powers a reason to treat more junior partners with respect.

In today's multi-polar world, this has become trickier and much more complicated.

Then there are the relationships with immediate neighbours which can often be tense. These need to be smoothed out, a modus vivendi reached on simmering or potentially explosive issues, a means of confidential communication established.

Instability next door can easily cross the border into your country. So how, without interfering in that other country, do you take avoiding action?

And then increasingly as the world splits into regions wanting to wield influence partly to mitigate big-power politics, there are the relationships that are regionally relevant.

All of these different facets of international relations need to be woven into a policy which is then pursued with consistency of purpose and commitment.

Ukraine has, rightly, prompted a recalibration of many nations' defence strategy. Finland and Sweden have joined NATO. Germany has increased defence spending significantly despite fiscal pressures. The transatlantic alliance has leapt back into life.

Immediate anxiety over Russia's present behaviour towards Ukraine has provoked a deeper worry about China's future behaviour, especially given the tensions over the status of Taiwan. This in turn must lead to a resurgent strategy on the part of the West to be prepared for all contingencies where China is concerned.

In 2022 and 2023 the West looked resolute. NATO was strengthened; the G7 announced a $600 billion programme of engagement with the developing world seeking to compete with the One Belt One Road plan of China; the USA stepped up its soft power push into Africa and South East Asia.

But then fatigue set in; interest waned. The Gaza conflict happened. Strategic focus became blurred. At the time of writing the fate of Ukraine hangs in the balance.

Yet the fact remains that if its fate mattered in early

2022, it matters more than ever two years further on. Not just Western allies but—as important—Western enemies will watch to see if the commitment shown at the beginning is a commitment shown until the end. If not, we will pay a much heavier price with a much larger commitment later.

As I often had cause to remark upon ruefully while in government, unfortunately, in politics and geopolitics, the crises don't come sequentially. They come on their own timetable which can be concurrent with other crises.

We presently have conflict in Eastern Europe and in the Middle East. We also face conflict in Africa, where there is a crisis in the Sudan and another in the Sahel—that clutch of nations across the north of Africa where the people are ravaged by the combined problems of poverty, exploding populations, poor institutions, extremism and bad governance. There is no one studying this situation who does not believe that Europe will face an influx of immigration and jihadism from the Sahel in the future. But the strategic will to act to stave off collapse and put the region on its feet is absent.

Then, apart from the crises, there is the need for consistency and coherence of approach to soft power. To give an example. We want the support of developing nations in the fight against climate change. But we also have to support their development, which inevitably involves those countries having better transport links, including airports and airlines, creating the necessary infrastructure, and so consuming more energy.

What those twin priorities mean in practice is that we should both help them to develop and do so in the most sustainable way possible. Underline the word "possible." If we refuse them investment for, say, natural gas projects they will burn either cheap coal or heavy diesel oil. At the same time, they will lose the funding gas would give them. The consequence will be that they don't develop. And that's something they will never accept. The reality is that gas is an essential transitional fuel. The EU now recognises this. But the investment gap was allowed to remain for too long, when two policies were operating not in alignment but in contradiction of one another, thus alienating key allies crucial for the broader Western strategy.

The point is policy needs to be devised strategically and with care; but then pursued with consistency of purpose and implementation.

Where the big risk comes is when foreign policy is pursued inconsistently, when events or issues are reacted to in an ad hoc way, when an awareness of the importance of clarity and coherence is neglected.

CHAPTER TWENTY-THREE

In Foreign Policy, Personal Relationships Are Built on Trust

In opposition, you can cherry-pick and, within reason, get away with loose language and positions on foreign policy. But in government, every relationship damaged by inconsiderate actions or statements can result in a real price paid by the country and you as a Leader.

By the same token, creating trust between Leaders can pay rich dividends. And once in government, you as Leader will find that trust is the currency of international relationships. If the currency is cheapened, it can harm your nation's interests—sometimes seriously; if it is valued, it can advance them. This can happen in small ways and large.

My good relationship with Italian Prime Minister Berlusconi—despite our very different politics and understandable anxiety about it among my advisers—turned out to be crucial in London winning the hotly contested bid to host the 2012 Olympics, when he switched Italian support from France to the UK.

My Home Secretary, David Blunkett, had a great relationship with his French opposite number—at the time Nicolas Sarkozy—though one was Labour and the other

Conservative. That sorted the refugee crisis at the Calais port, at least for a while.

Anyone who has been a prime minister or president would be able to give similar examples of where political friendships—even across the normal political divides—have proved vital in advancing national interests.

Sometimes the relationships in foreign policy exist already and the task is to nurture them. Other times, the relationships have to be built. And here it is important to say how foreign policy should not be conducted.

Government is not an NGO. The Leader is not an activist. You are not leading a pressure group speaking their truth to power. As Leader you are the power. And it is a duty of a government to protect and enhance its country's interests. Yes, its country's values, too. But that is easy to say and frequently hard to do.

When I was in opposition, I foolishly allowed my party to say that in government we would pursue an "ethical foreign policy." And who would want to pursue an "unethical foreign policy"?!

But the reason it was foolish is that it implied a standard of morality that is completely inconsistent with the conduct of a country's affairs in the real world.

Needless to say, once in government, I realised the standard couldn't be maintained. The retreat from it was an embarrassment. But the mistake wasn't the retreat; it was the enunciation of a policy that had no chance of surviving contact with grown-up politics.

There are important countries with whom a Leader will have to deal, who may do things public opinion in your own nation disapproves of—or that you the Leader disagree with. These usually concern human rights issues—and more often it is Western countries that face this dilemma, though not always.

You need to have your stance right from the beginning.

If it is in your country's interests to engage and have friendly relations with another country—and these interests could be economic, but they could also be to do with security, or with that other country's ability to affect issues which concern your country—your job is to make the engagement happen and work.

You will be criticised at home but that comes with the job and can never be a reason for failing to do your duty.

If there are areas of disagreement with that other country, raise them. No harm in that. And maybe some good will come of it. But do it in a way that doesn't imperil the relationship.

Now naturally there may be countries that do something so egregious or detrimental to your values that they also damage your interests. So the calculus of those interests changes. Russia's invasion of Ukraine is a good example.

But the point is: foreign policy is a hard-headed not a soft-hearted business, in which relations of trust need to be built and maintained even when politically difficult to do so.

For example, in the case of Saudi Arabia there is no doubt about the things with which we disagree. But there is equally no doubt that the new leadership is pursuing the most ambitious programme of reform and modernisation the country has ever seen, with a virtual social revolution taking place.

This change will fundamentally affect the region and to a degree the world, in ways which are positive for our security and the global economy.

It was awkward when the Biden administration had to back down from its initial position of hostility to the new Saudi leadership and engage with it. But it should never have been in that position in the first place, not because criticism of human rights abuses, or condemnation of the terrible murder of Jamal Khashoggi, was wrong but because that criticism shouldn't have obliterated the things happening on the other side of the ledger that were good, worthy of support and hugely in American interests.

So, President Biden was right to change tack.

In doing so, he wasn't putting interests before values but accepting that to defend those values and those interests, he had to take a balanced and hard-headed approach to the conduct of foreign policy.

Failure to have done so would have alienated an ally and pushed that ally further towards China, something which would be directly contrary to America's interests and values. An NGO isn't obliged to deal with those nuances of what is ethical. The Leader of a nation is.

So, it is important to think through the implications of each important position you take as a Leader.

It is vital, too, never to forget that the Leader you're dealing with is also human. And at a certain level, the relationship you forge with them is very much like a friendship.

The other Leader must know that if you give your word, it will be kept; that if they make an agreement with you,

you will stick to it; or that delicate matters which should remain confidential don't turn up in your media in a disobliging way.

When half a century and more ago, Henry Kissinger as national security adviser and Richard Nixon as president of the USA were engaged in the immensely sensitive opening to China after years of complete diplomatic isolation from each other, they had to act with subtlety, insight, wisdom and understanding. But they also had to build trust. Confidences were kept. Each tried to help the other. Personal relationships were created, not least between Kissinger and Zhou Enlai.

At crucial times, each had to give their word and each had to honour it. And eventually trust came into being and agreements could be made.

That trust was preconditional to the breakthrough. Without it, the necessary step forward might never have happened or happened much later. And I believe the thaw in the relationship between China and America was also significant in China's leadership enlarging their perspective and seeing how a capitalist nation and markets could have advantages.

At a nation-to-nation level, Leader to Leader, political affiliation, the other country's internal politics, don't really matter. What matters is that you can have frank conversations about things which are important for one or the other or both of you.

The reason why maintaining good relations is tricky is that you may be dealing with an issue where your politics and the other Leader's politics are in contradiction. In fact, they often are. Your public opinion is pushing one way; theirs in the opposite direction.

A Leader has to be smart enough to recognise this and strong enough to take account of it. Always understand: the other side has its politics. If you disrespect that or dismiss it because it's inconvenient to yours, you make a big mistake. That is where the trust is lost, and it is a very long road back.

Leaders hate to see other Leaders grandstanding, even if they do a fair amount of it themselves. Occasionally you need to; but do it only out of necessity and recognise the price you will pay.

Trust is the currency of international diplomacy. Build it up, and use it wisely.

CHAPTER TWENTY-FOUR

Navigating the Straits Between the USA and China (and Don't Forget India)

Most of this book explores general principles of governing. But there is one specific shift in twenty-first-century geopolitics that deserves individual attention, and that is the relationship between the USA and China. America is many countries' principal security partner, is the world's strongest economy, has the world's foremost language of choice and much of the world's popular culture, and carries a large heft of traditional experience in global affairs. China is almost every country's largest trading partner, after their nearest neighbour. Talk to virtually any Leader today, and very soon up comes the topic of navigation between these two giants.

For years, certainly when I was in office, there were high, though in retrospect naive, hopes of a happy ending to the rise of China: "In the end, don't worry, they will become like us."

We're not at the end, of course, and that should not be forgotten; but right now, and for the foreseeable future, China is not like us and shows no indication of becoming so. If anything, the signs point in the opposite direction.

America, after some dithering, as is its wont, has fully

woken up to the "threat" posed by China. Indeed, it is probably the one issue that unites what is otherwise a fractured political scene. The USA, therefore, is taking measures month by month that all carry the same basic message: the USA and China are locked in a great power competition and America had better win.

There was a time when America would say to countries—allies and neutrals—"Look, we understand, you're doing business with China; it's fine—we get it, carry on; but be careful, keep us informed, and now let's talk about something else." These days, the USA doesn't want to talk about something else, it wants to talk about this. And in clear—even mildly menacing—terms.

So, we have a situation where the economic ties with China are real and, for many nations, seemingly irreplaceable; and US pressure not to engage with China is likewise real and seemingly irreducible.

China has dropped its "quietly, quietly" approach to diplomacy in favour of a "dare to win" mantra that has, not unnaturally, severely jolted America into not only waking up but getting the equivalent of an intravenous drip of caffeine shoved into its political veins.

The American trade with China is still vast—many hundreds of billions of dollars. But it is now subject to policy-imposed headwinds. In areas of security sensitivity or even industrial competitiveness, the USA is applying tough tariffs and, in particular, is now throttling or attempting to throttle China's access to the advanced computer chips vital for higher-end AI.

The current technological revolution is creating a whole

new field of competition in which the stakes are incredibly high and on which neither side believes it can afford to lose.

In addition, global conflict, notably the war in Ukraine, has created a burgeoning alliance between China and Russia, with Iran and North Korea sometimes lining up alongside them, which has resulted in opposition to the American/ Western position on virtually any major flashpoint of geo- politics, a situation which then effectively paralyses the United Nations Security Council, which was not in great shape to begin with.

Now, all the above needs some qualification, or at least some caution in thinking the nature of the USA–China rela- tionship is immutably destined to stay hostile or even descend into military conflict.

The USA, for its part, will reserve some space for co- operation while engaging in competition and occasional confrontation. It will do so out of necessity. There is no major global challenge today, from dealing with pandem- ics, to climate change, to the world's economic stability, which does not require China's active participation to resolve it.

So, the rest of the world watches this complex geopolit- ical dance and tries to calculate its own way around the dance floor, without bumping too hard into either partner.

That process of navigation, which was tricky a couple of years ago, is now likely to be even trickier. Leaders there- fore need a strategy to handle it, recognising that their own influence over the issue is—except for a very few nations— unfortunately negligible.

First things first: treat the issue as requiring its own

special plan. Think carefully of the ground to camp on, i.e., the parameters and principles governing your nation's relationship with both powers. Maybe one is a relationship of necessity, one of inclination. Usually, China will fit into the first category, the USA the second. Or maybe you genuinely want equidistance, though be mindful of the dangers of ending up offending both parties. The point is, for these purposes, you need a strategy, not an ad hoc lurching from one position to another.

Understand how other geopolitical players will position themselves, because that may affect your position.

For example, whatever you may hear to the contrary, Europe will ultimately go with the Americans. They won't like doing so at times, and they may play around with not doing it, but don't be fooled. The invasion of Ukraine by Putin, and the closeness between the Russian and Chinese leaderships, has removed any ambiguity of a deep nature. Europe will line up with the USA, as will such other traditional American allies as Australia and Japan. So that has to be factored into the strategic calculation.

Despite the short-term risk of isolationism, over time the USA will start to be much more active around the world in pursuit of the winning goal. In Africa we see this happening already. In the Middle East, where the conventional thinking is that the USA has vacated the space, allowing China to move in, America will re-engage and will, if the price of renewed power domination in that region is a security guarantee to nations worried particularly about Iran, give that guarantee, maybe not quite in a NATO Article 5 form (whereby an attack on one is seen as an attack on all), but something reasonably bankable. In Asia, it will understand the mistake it made in leaving trade negotiations to founder and will reinvigorate them.

That doesn't mean China will retreat or stand still. On the contrary, it will move up several gears, building on economic ties, and possibly starting to export technology solutions as its willingness to use data in ways the West finds unacceptable gains it an edge. The Chinese won't apply pressure as overtly as the Americans; their approach will be more subtle. It will be a version of "no strings; do whatever you like within your own borders," no "tiresome" lectures on human rights, the ostensible rejection of American "arrogance," and, in contrast to Western bureaucracy constantly tripping up Western efficacy, the promise of speed of action. A Leader needs to understand, though, that "strings" come in many forms—and not all with a "human rights" tag.

Over time China will begin to feel the burden of playing the geopolitical game at the highest level. It can be a Big Dog by all means; but remember the Big Dog is usually blamed by the little dogs. Power is a responsibility and China will find out soon what that means.

Amid this great power tension, regional and continental alliances—the European Union, ASEAN, the African Union, the developing groupings in Latin America—will become of increasing importance. What nations struggle to do alone, they may achieve together. Strategies held or fashioned in common, united positions that collectively have the weight to make both giants pause or tread carefully, making the competition between the two also a platform for advantage, for extracting the best deal, the most credible assurances, the least breakable promises—this approach will gain traction.

Remember, the advantage of great power competition for everyone else is that—to a degree—the great powers are also looking to persuade, entice and prompt nations to join their "side." This can yield an opportunity to keep both sweet. But bear in mind it is *to a degree*. Play that hand with care. Don't overplay it.

Finally, it needs to be borne in mind that the USA and China are not the only major players in town. India is on the march. It has the world's biggest population. It has fantastic technology, energetic youth, a culture that is bursting with colour and creativity. Once two superpowers become three, lots of opportunities for countries to engage in smart diplomacy are created.

The population aspect of all this is interesting. It's interesting in general terms, because the world's population is set to start shrinking, giving rise to the complete opposite of the challenge the world thought it had, namely too large a population. And it's interesting in country-by-country terms, because, if current trends continue, this depopulation will not be evenly spread. The population of China is set to decline quite dramatically—to around 800 million over the next decades. The population of India will soar to 1.5 billion, making it far and away the largest in the world. This is bound to have major great power consequences.

So, a Leader taking a long-term view of their country's interests, should regard building the relationship with India as an indispensable part of a modern foreign policy.

But more immediately, we should not assume that American or Chinese politics will stay static.

American politics—wildly fragmented and unpredictable as it may currently be—may settle down again. The Chinese leadership, which looks all-powerful, may find the limits of its power manifested. An experiment in Leninist central control, which I would say has never proved sustainable anywhere, may not yield China, with its diverse population and thriving middle class, as an exception but rather return it to the rule.

The importance of this rivalry between these two superpowers and how it affects other countries means a Leader cannot afford to stumble into a position on it, but must frame it with thought and care.

CHAPTER TWENTY-FIVE

Foreign Policy Is Becoming
Domestic Policy

The navigation challenge between America and China underlines the degree to which foreign policy is affecting domestic policy.

To a degree foreign policy has always had the capacity to affect domestic politics. Even in calm geopolitical times it matters. There are Leaders to see. International issues which even if they don't have massive domestic impact immediately, can, if ignored, come to do so. Hitherto largely unnoticed disputes with other nations which need settling. All these are things which may not hit the headlines, but they can hit the smooth conduct of government business.

You realise as a Leader that how your country is seen externally does actually matter internally because it plays back into your politics. Before you're in government, no one much cares what you as a potential Leader may think and you have, usually, very limited knowledge. Once you're in government, suddenly there is a whole list of new partnerships and relationships which need to be managed, built and tended to.

However, in recent times, the conduct of foreign policy has moved from being usually of second or even third order importance in domestic politics, to having the potential to become first order.

There was a time when foreign ministers would float benignly above the scrappy melee of the politics of everyday living. They would spend large amounts of time abroad attending dignified gatherings where politicians exchange positions on issues with politeness and elegance, returning every so often to report to a parliament all too willing to be patronised as the minister would regale it with tales of places and people with unpronounceable names about which the members had to feign interest in order to appear worldly.

OK, some might have had a particular interest in a particular country or issue, but by and large that would rarely impinge on the purview of the Leader. Global issues tended not to impinge on the electorate, either, unless they were of such significance that they affected domestic policy or were to do with local differences with immediate neighbours.

External politics, in other words, mattered much less than internal.

This is changing.

The USA–China rivalry is one factor.

The Ukraine war is another, because of its scale and impact on supply chains of grain and fertiliser; and for less obvious reasons, because it has upset our assumptions about modern conflict.

A full-scale war—mid-twentieth-century in nature between two competing conventional armies with hundreds of thousands of casualties right on the border of the European Union—was unthinkable a few years ago. Now it is a reality. The aggressor is a United Nations Security Council permanent member.

It has been supported in the aggression by China, which has become much more assertive or aggressive, depending on your viewpoint.

And through the conflict, a new alliance has sprung into being between Russia and Iran; and then, even more bizarrely, between Russia and North Korea.

So, perceptibly and unmistakably, a club has been formed: China, Russia, Iran and North Korea.

It is a club without a long waiting list. But it nevertheless includes two nuclear powers and two aspirant nuclear powers, the world's second largest economy and largest country by land mass, one Islamic republic and the world's most isolated and unpredictable dictatorship.

It is not a club of equals. And it is not one in which the Chinese will want to be parked in. China is much more powerful, more sophisticated and far-sighted than the other members of its current circle, and even though it proclaims that the alliance with Russia is "without limits," it will in reality make those limits very clear, albeit privately.

China's current position, though, leads to a paradox in Western policy.

As we have seen, China and America are now in open confrontation and competition.

America sees China as its biggest threat. And by dint of size and weight, it is. But America also believes—as do the rest of us, even if it is an unspoken belief—that China alone of the club members can be expected to have a significant interest in stability and a significant aversion to unpredictability.

Therefore, to a degree and paradoxically, we rely on China to constrain the tendency towards instability and unpredictability on the part of the other countries with which it is currently aligned.

It was China that took the use of tactical nuclear weapons by Russia off the table early in the Ukraine conflict. It is China that supports efforts to prevent escalation of the Gaza war. And China alone has the capability of taming the wildness of the North Korean despot.

At least we hope all this is so.

But the shock of what Russia has done, the forming of this extraordinary club, China's turn towards heavy-handed Leninist leadership, combined with its determination to return Taiwan to mainland Chinese control, means that for Western countries today, belief and hope are risky guides to policy.

We may hope China does not go rogue on us. We may believe it won't; but we can no longer form policy wisely on this basis.

The mood in the West will, therefore, come back to a familiar lesson from history: to achieve peace, prepare for war.

The conflict in Gaza has been very different in origin and nature. However, it too has repercussions that are not only global but that affect the domestic politics of nations.

Quite apart from the immediate and tragic impact of the conflict on Israelis and Palestinians, it has fuelled division and resentment more widely. Division inside the West, as local Muslim populations have combined with (usually leftist) traditional political elements to attack the Western governments' (predominantly) pro-Israel stance. Division between the West and the global Muslim community. Resentment at what are perceived or regularly claimed as "double standards" of Western policy. Western public opinion is itself divided, not simply about the conflict but about the place of Muslim communities within Western society.

It needs to be borne in mind, too, that whereas a lot of Western commentary sees the Arab world and wider Middle East as anti-Israel and unified in their support of the Palestinian cause, the reality is more nuanced. There is huge support for Palestinian statehood, but underneath the surface there is also deep ambivalence about the role of the Muslim Brotherhood (Hamas being part of that movement) in that cause. And there is a profound distrust and fear of the Islamic Republic of Iran.

And as it becomes clear that—as with Gaza—the Sunni Muslim Brotherhood and the Shia Islamic Republic are prepared to work together, this ambivalence grows.

Increasingly across the region, there is—often understated—a clear distinction being made between Islam and Islamism, between the religion and the distortion of it into a political ideology.

This distinction is also entering the internal politics of Western countries. The West, up to now, has been quite successfully persuaded that "Islamophobia" is the same as anxiety about the integration of Muslim communities into Western society.

But the Gaza conflict has heightened unease among the

host populations in Western countries about the degree to which their Muslim communities have become influenced by Islamist thinking. This will deepen.

Political parties, especially those on the left, will worry about the electoral impact of pro-Palestinian protesters on their vote should they not take a robust enough stance in favour of the Palestinian cause; the rest of the population will be wary of the existence within those protests of Islamist groups; and this will push politics to the right unless the parties from the progressive wing of politics find the correct political balance to strike.

On the other hand, there are increasing numbers of voices in the Muslim world fighting back against the attempt to politicise their religion, and they could find common cause with those in Western countries worried about the influence of Islamism. Both will believe that a just and reasonable solution to the Palestinian–Israeli conflict is in their mutual interests.

So, there are many different layers of complexity to the politics of this issue, but there is no doubt that it has, nonetheless, the potential directly to affect a nation's internal politics.

The point is that whether it is tension between the USA and China, the war in Ukraine or the conflict in Gaza, all are feeding into the domestic agenda of nations irrespective of those nations' direct involvement in them.

This melding of the foreign and the domestic will increase as the world shifts, as has just been described, from two superpowers to three—the USA, China and India—by the middle of the century.

For the first time in modern history, Western nations will not dominate global politics. Like it or not we will live in a multi-polar world. The West may fear this; the "club" will rejoice in it; some "neutral" nations may welcome it and some not. But there are profound implications for Leaders devising foreign policy.

The world may go multi-polar, but for the West in general and the USA in particular, things won't stop there. Because one of the poles is a club that is outright hostile to the West, it will also be necessary to discuss how best to combat it.

This debate and the different positions taken by parties and Leaders will influence quite substantially the outcome of domestic politics.

And as a consequence of this Great Power/East–West rivalry, other countries will be forced to adopt their own strategy towards it. In doing so, they will want to assess what will be the policy changes they can expect from Western countries.

I would say "neutral" countries can expect the following:

- Western nations will beef up their defence capabilities, and defence policy will become a much more active part of domestic policy.
- There will be a deep dive into what modern defence capability looks like, given developments in technology especially around drones; and a big emphasis on cyber defensive and offensive capacity.
- Western nations will believe that technological superiority over China is a "must" and will do what is necessary to achieve it.

- India will be wooed by everyone. India's policy will be India First. But the rest of the world will increasingly ask what that means for them and will want answers.
- The West at some point will start correcting the immense bureaucratic flaws that hinder its support for the developing world, and begin utilising its immense advantages, not least in the private sector.
- The international system—UN, WTO, World Bank, IMF—will come under intense strain because of geopolitical rivalry.
- Trade will become a weapon of choice, with potentially damaging consequences for the global economy.
- For issues requiring global cooperation—climate, health, etc.—there will be a tension between the acceptance that action on a global scale is necessary and the anxiety that such action will involve individual players losing the competitive edge.
- The West will start to take a much more pragmatic approach to foreign policy.
- A recognition will develop that the distinction between Islam and Islamism is a critical fulcrum for policy and allies.

The effect of all this will be to make foreign policy a much more complicated business, requiring strategic grip, deep analysis, and situational awareness on a larger scale and at a greater level of sophistication than most countries, up to now, have needed.

Foreign ministers will no longer be flying at high altitude, looking down on the rough political terrain below, but will be observing it at close quarters, in a vehicle with their political Leaders sitting alongside them and frequently taking the wheel.

CHAPTER TWENTY-SIX

How to Negotiate

I almost called this chapter "How to Conduct a Meeting," because a skill worth learning all on its own is how you make a meeting productive, how you manage its flow and guide its path to arrive at the desired outcome.

However, the meetings that matter are those in which you have a specific aim. And that involves a negotiation. Or at a minimum a circumnavigation. A requirement not merely to have an objective, but the necessity of a strategy to achieve it.

Leadership is a constant process of negotiation. It begins with knowing what you want. Your strategic goal must be absolutely clear—to you, but not necessarily and sometimes not desirably to those with whom you're negotiating.

That sounds obvious, but often I come across Leaders who approach an important meeting with only a vague idea of what it is they want out of it. The result is usually a nothing.

You need to know with precision. That way, you can be diverted, the meeting can go down dark or blind alleys, the formalities can intrude on the substance, the goal seemingly obscured by irrelevancies, but you can find a path back—if you're clear enough about where it is you want to go.

Of course, negotiations come in all different shapes and

sizes. Sometimes it's a simple demand and the answer is a yes or no. In such cases, unless you're confident of a positive answer, you have to consider what it is the other party may want from you or consider something you might offer in exchange for the favour you're asking.

Put yourself in their shoes. Will they think that you have a close enough relationship that they're prepared to yield just because it is you who is asking? Then ask yourself whether you have ever built on that relationship and if not, why not. Also ask yourself whether, if you were them, you would be inclined to give, and what might make you so inclined.

Suppose you conclude during the meeting that the answer will be a negative one. For whatever reason, they're not going to give what you want. How do you end that meeting without embarrassment, without them feeling they have let you down, even if they have? The chances are that this won't be the only negotiation with them, or it may be that time and circumstance could reopen the same negotiation more favourably.

In such instances you need to find a way of ending the meeting gracefully, in a way which preserves or even creates goodwill, suggesting possibly a period of further reflection, or keeping of the matter under advisement, or just showing understanding of the reasons for refusal.

Another lesson I learnt in politics: a good meeting is where you have spoken less than the other person.

Get them to talk first. Get them to open up. The most important factor in any meeting is knowing when to keep quiet. Allow them full rein to speak and therefore to reveal.

This can be crucial as you adjust tactics in the course of

the meeting. You may have thought the key to success was their attitude to x but it turns out it was really y.

I learnt a lot of these lessons conducting the Northern Ireland peace process. We were fortunate that I could spend the time on it. The parties—after we got past the preliminary unburdening of historical positions—were prepared to listen to the concerns of the other. Over time, the fixed and absolutist positions yielded to a recognition that there were true, mutual interests, which meant compromise was not regarded as betrayal. I had a great partner in the Irish prime minister. And we were patient, hearing everyone out over a prolonged period. In addition, each meeting and negotiation had a clear point to it, which helped remove the innumerable obstacles to a final agreement.

During the past two decades, I have been engaged in negotiations over the Middle East peace process around the Israeli–Palestinian conflict. For most of that time, frankly, there has been little process and only sporadic peace. And the contrast with Northern Ireland is instructive.

The negotiations in the Middle East have involved the two principal parties—but also the wider region, the USA, Europe, virtually every country with an opinion on the issue, and that is most of the world.

There are many reasons why this "peace process" is difficult. But one of them is that almost all the guidelines set out above have never applied.

Each party is convinced that only they really understand the other and they absolutely don't. So, rather than putting themselves in the other's shoes, they wield a huge shoehorn to try to force their own shoe on the other's foot.

Meetings tend to focus on matters either too large to ensure the meeting has a precise objective, or too small to make it worth top-level engagement from the parties or the international community.

The Americans lead the negotiations fitfully, sometimes super engaged, other times somewhat detached, but to be fair it's unreasonable to expect them to be otherwise given all the different calls on their time and political bandwidth.

Countries with some influence use/abuse the issue within their own politics, which often means subsequent negotiations in which they participate start in a poor spirit.

The degree of trust between the parties themselves is negligible. Therefore, they're never sure the negotiation is worth it.

And above all, the negotiations have never really got to the heart of the matter, because that would involve a sustained level of thought and commitment not just from the parties at the centre of it all but the international community, which, given the turnover in leadership internationally, is hardly likely.

Believe it or not, I still think this peace process can ultimately succeed—because there are new forces in the region, who will commit the time and energy, and because the Gaza conflict has brought home to the parties the impossibility of managing the issue rather than solving it.

And then these lessons of how to negotiate will be essential. But this is a subject, outside the scope of this book, which deserves treatment in its own right.

In negotiations, occasionally, it is right to threaten, to go brutal. But here is another big lesson. You can threaten. But misread the psychology of the person you're threatening or make an empty threat and that is fatal.

An example of doing it right would be the way President Kennedy handled the Cuban Missile Crisis. He made a threat. It was credible. But he also had the ingenuity and skill to create a relationship with Khrushchev which meant that he could nonetheless negotiate a deal which averted war.

An example of doing it wrong—fortunately in a much less critical negotiation—I recall as a young and upcoming frontbench Treasury opposition spokesman, when I was part of a delegation sent to Washington, DC to argue a tax point against the US administration. We met the Treasury secretary, the formidable James Baker. Overreaching way out of my league, I threatened that if our demand was not met, there would be retaliation against the USA by the British Parliament. At which point, he laid out with brutal clarity the counter-retaliation the administration would take. Needless to say, I had got out a pea-shooter and he held a bazooka. I retreated red-faced.

Honey is better than vinegar unless you're tossing lettuce leaves for a salad.

Never lose your cool. It's demeaning and doesn't work.

When the other side is talking nonsense, consider whether it is worth pointing it out or whether there are bigger things you need to argue about. If they have a grievance, irrespective of whether you think it's justified, hear them out. Let them get it off their chest.

So, draw the other out. If you know it's going to be a tricky negotiation, begin above your bottom line so you can offer a concession at the appropriate moment to close the deal.

Think of the meeting format. The system—for completely understandable and good reasons—detests a one-on-one between Leaders. They want a record kept. They want to know what has been agreed and why.

But relationships of strength between Leaders are rarely created by two Leaders sitting opposite each other with phalanxes of officials on either side. The other Leader may be anxious about speaking freely; he or she may at this point not want an "accurate record." They want to open their heart, explain their difficulties, explore your appetite for making it easy or hard for them.

Or the format might include just the closest advisers. The point is to think through what set-up will work best. Negotiations aren't legal process. They're as much subjective as objective. They're about the feel, the spirit, the relationship, about picking the right moment to strike for the finish.

Learning when to close, knowing when the right moment has arrived, is of vital importance, as I found during the tortuous Northern Ireland negotiations for the Good Friday Agreement—the founding document for the peace, in 1998. Judging it correctly then was literally the difference between success and failure.

Zero-sum games are rarely productive in politics. In Northern Ireland we finally managed to escape that bind, which was crucial in making progress. Contrast that with the Middle East, where things remain mired in zero-sum dynamics.

Ultimately, the best negotiations are always those which

leave the other side with a sense of achievement. Both sides happy is the best outcome. Anything which looks like a big victory for you at the expense of the other will be a pyrrhic victory, leaving a bad taste in the mouth of the other, for which you will pay in the future.

Even if you're delighted, even if you believe you have outmanoeuvred the other side, run rings round them, think you've been smart and they've been dumb, never show it. Don't let your people show it. Be content with the result.

Negotiation is not a science. It is an art.

PART VI

Communications in a New Media Environment

CHAPTER TWENTY-SEVEN

Strategic Communication: The Difference Between a Narrative and a Press Release

In many walks of life, communicating simply means informing people, telling them what you're doing, imparting knowledge. But in politics, it is both a science and an art that can make the difference between success and failure.

It is vital to distinguish between tactical communications and strategic communications. Tactical are the press releases, the announcements of everyday government existence, the "what." Strategic is the story you're telling about the "why."

The former need not concern us. Anyone with a reasonably professional approach can do it. And it has its place. However, where true political skill lies is in mastery of the strategic.

Government Leaders need a narrative, one that explains why you are, and why you deserve to be, in government; something that expresses not only what you're doing but also the values, sentiments and motives behind doing it.

This narrative is important at any time, but especially important for the change-maker. It sets out why you are challenging the status quo, why you might be asking people to accept difficult things—things that will make you opponents as well as friends. It tells a story, not simply a collection of facts or more often claims.

I liken governing to leading people on a journey. You don't just begin by stepping out. You begin with a description of a destination—the house on the hill, you might call it. And you tell the people: that's where we're heading because in that house are many good things, things that will improve and enrich our lives, make the journey worth it.

It's vital to describe the destination because the journey is not going to be easy: there will be obstacles and dangers and pitfalls and diversions that shake people's faith and make them wonder why they embarked on it in the first place.

Think of Moses and the Exodus from Egypt. You might have thought that since he was leading his people out of slavery and oppression, they would have been perpetually grateful. But they weren't. They complained bitterly much of the time. They dissented. They rebelled. They frequently averred that they would have been better off if he had just left them where they were. The waters of Meribah (when Moses struck the rock to bring forth water after the quarrelling of the people about his leadership) were as vivid for them as the parting of the Red Sea.

Moses had to put up with the "stiff-necked" attitude of the people. But he also countered it by continually explaining that he was leading them to a land of "milk and honey" where their every need would be better fulfilled. Of course, he got a bit of help from God, who sent manna from heaven. Unfortunately, that's not something your everyday Leader can rely on.

What all this means for the modern Leader is that every time their government is announcing something significant, it must announce the "why" and not just the "what." Strategic communications is like a washing line running the length of the government—as my colleague Peter Mandelson used to say. Each individual policy or initiative must be attached to the line like an item of clothing.

That line is the narrative. And it must be carefully constructed. If it is weak, or inadequate, if it frays easily, or is poorly attached to firm poles of conviction and understanding, then very soon the government appears to the people as if it's not so much striding towards a destination as merely walking round in circles.

The importance of narrative can be well illustrated by considering the countries that joined the European Union after the fall of the Berlin Wall. All of them were former Communist states. All of them therefore had non-existent or inefficient private sectors, bloated public sectors, and little or no experience of governing in a culture of democracy.

Poland and Ukraine were at that time two broadly comparable countries, with roughly the same prospects in a post-Communist world. But fast-forward to 2021—before the war in Ukraine—and the contrast had become stark. In the thirty years or so after 1989, Poland had become prosperous and vibrant. Many of its people, who for the first couple of decades after the break-up of the Soviet Union had moved to other parts of Europe in search of jobs and prosperity, started to return to a country where there was now a clear opportunity to get on.

Ukraine, by contrast, had been beset by constant

problems of politics and governance and fallen significantly behind its neighbour.

The difference in the two countries' fortunes could be measured in average earnings: in 2021, incomes in Poland were around twice those in Ukraine. Sure, Poland has experienced well-documented challenges in its democracy. Some Poles, I'm sure, would dispute the generally rosy picture I paint. But by any objective standards the last decades have been good for Poland and disappointing for Ukraine.

Poland succeeded, in large part, because the prospect and then reality of membership of the European Union gave its political leadership a visible and attractive "house on the hill." It was the same prospect for many other Eastern European states. People could see the journey, with all its challenges, was worth the effort.

All the countries had to prove eligibility for membership by implementing reform programmes. These meant huge and often painful changes to the status quo, but the leadership was able to convince the people that the benefits outweighed the costs.

Today, countries like Albania that are queuing up to join the EU use the same story to drive the reform that is required to gain membership. After the war, Ukraine—if it gets a clear path to European Union membership—will, with the right leadership, move much faster towards the changes which eluded it while Poland was advancing.

All countries need a story. Sometimes it isn't as plain as that of Poland. But the principle is the same.

When I first ran for office in 1997, we had a slogan: New Labour, New Britain. It was straightforward, uncomplicated and got across the message we wanted to convey. After four election defeats in a row, my party had learnt its lesson and had changed. Britain as it approached a new century with a stale old establishment in power needed renewal also. We were the people who had modernised our party and would modernise the country.

Not everyone liked the slogan. Some hated it. But no one misunderstood it.

Today, across the Middle East, the countries making most progress are those with Leaders who send a clear message to their own people of a positive vision for the future of their country, even if it is not a democracy. Those countries driving modernisation across the region are succeeding, in part because each leadership's communication with its own people is clear: we're on a journey of change because our youth can't be held back by introspective culture but need to be connected to the world; and our economy must diversify because dependence on fossil fuel is no longer wise or acceptable. Our enemy is extremism; our ally is tolerance.

Their narrative is one of unashamed modernisation. It places religious belief in an individual and social setting, not a political one, rejecting the use of religion as political ideology. It embraces technology as a route to economic diversification but also connectivity. It is easy to understand and easy to convey.

In some African countries today Leaders are striking out with a new narrative which, in time, will be very effective: let's stop debating the colonial past, let's set aside the dependence on Western largesse and aid, and instead let's stand on our own two feet, adding value to the commodities we have in abundance, leapfrogging the Western legacy systems through the use of technology, and sorting out the corruption which holds us back. It's a narrative of independence, of self-reliance, of taking responsibility for your future, not leaving it to the generosity of others, which is never large or reliable enough. And it will chime with a young population on their smartphones.

The challenge of Western democracy at present is the lack of a clear narrative. We want to return to high levels of growth and rising living standards, but it is not clear how. We know the geopolitics of the world is changing and Western powers will no longer be in sole command, but we're not sure where that leaves us.

We have to recover a sense of mission which, to my mind, will be focused on harnessing the twenty-first-century technological revolution; and to revive confidence in democracy by showing it can deliver not only for us but for the developing world.

But, for these purposes, the point is simply to emphasise that the absence of the narrative creates a situation where necessary reform is harder and leadership seems to drift, uncertain of destination or a path to it.

When working with governments round the world, one of the first things my institute does is to help them craft their narrative. This needs careful thought.

The narrative must be strong enough to endure and be robust. It has to be one the Leader's supporters believe in and share. It must be capable of being expressed in plain language, not fancy political speak. It can't be loose or fuzzy. Simplicity is a virtue. There may be all manner of complexity behind it, and buttressing it, but the narrative itself has to be easy to grasp.

Once that narrative has been created, it's not enough for the Leader to carry the burden of communicating it on their own. They must get everyone in the government ranks to do so. Every minister, every person speaking on behalf of the government, must get it and do it.

A minister has an announcement to make. Ensure that when they announce, they explain: this is what we're doing, and this is why we're doing it. Here's the problem, and here's the solution.

If this happens, it doesn't make the opposition to reform or change disappear, but it does force it to respond to the narrative and not just to the announcement. If you make the case for "why," they are obliged to explain "why not."

The clarity of narrative is even more important in the era of social media. But in the end, social media won't decide whether you win or lose. Delivery will. Especially if connected to a strong story about not just what you have done or will do in government, but why.

CHAPTER TWENTY-EIGHT

How to Handle Criticism, Twenty-first-Century Style

How many "normal" politicians can you think of? No, seriously. How many come across as well adjusted, essentially grounded, individuals, who behave and act like the people you want to spend time with, would go to for personal advice, would trust with your inner secrets?

Not many and, increasingly, not many at all near the top.

Politicians have, of course, always invited criticism. Read some of the things said about Abraham Lincoln during his presidential campaign or Churchill during his long estrangement from the British establishment in the 1930s. Or amuse yourself by reading the coffee-shop literature in the time of the early-eighteenth-century English essayist Joseph Addison—scurrilous, defamatory, abusive and unreasonable.

But our era has seen criticism taken to a whole new level. The prevalence and reach of media—social and conventional—has turned it into a weapon of psychological warfare, a bludgeon, a brutal, merciless source of persecution. Criticism is now not the simple making of an unfavourable judgement or an unforgiving analysis of error, presumed or real. It has become a sort of contest for attention, where reflective javelin-throwers, who take the time to ensure their projectiles are carefully smoothed and weighted for accuracy in flight, are outcompeted by those who hurl rough-hewed, nasty, hastily assembled javelins of disapproval, that go higher and faster, targeting anything in their path, and more likely to get noticed by onlookers.

It is true that one benefit of the media fragmentation we have witnessed over the past few years is that new forms of intelligent engagement can enter the lists. Podcasts, for example, have on the whole proved themselves to be a reasonable medium for reasonable people. But such enterprises have been swamped in scale by the noisy clatter of the shrill and the shrieking.

The risk for politics is substantial. "Normal" folk like neither to give nor to receive such blows aimed at destroying peace of mind, provoking deepest concealed insecurities, ruining the individual's capacity to think straight or at least consistently and clearly. Criticism "gets" them. Why wouldn't it? You're normal. If people are unpleasant to you, you feel it. It hurts. It gnaws away. It distracts and deters. If you think you're being unfairly castigated—and you often are in politics—that dampens and dismays your spirit. Unless you are possessed of extraordinary courage, you think twice before stepping forward.

All too often, therefore, the political arena these days is left to the chronically insensitive and the populists. Both groups are of the unusual character that gains some strange form of sustenance from abuse, that covets it. They know it stimulates in their own supporters the necessary feeling of being under siege, a feeling that then boosts the populists'

sway over them, and protects them against charges both justified and unjustified.

For those not so constituted, but who are sufficiently
excited and motivated to make political leadership their
goal, the only solution is to grow a mental carapace, a shell
inside which you can achieve a Zen-like meditative state.
That doesn't mean you're ignoring the criticism that comes
your way—you can't—or that you refuse to acknowledge its
existence—you won't—but you're able to view it from a
zone of detachment.

I once asked the former prime minister of Singapore Lee
Kuan Yew how he coped with stress. I rather expected him—
being the sort of tough, no-nonsense Leader he was—to give
me a suitably dismissive "buck yourself up" response. Instead,
he told me that as he had grown older, he had embarked on
a programme of meditation and that he had found it immeasur-
ably useful. On talking to other Leaders, I found the use of
meditation among them surprisingly common.

I myself came to it late in life, and even now I am not sure
that, according to the strict definition of the term, I do medi-
tate. But I think I do. For me, it is just a quiet time, a time
of letting go all negative thoughts, a moment of appreciation
of your smallness and insignificance in the grand scheme of
things, but not in your own life or in the lives of those near
and dear to you.

It's during that time that I recall the words of Niebuhr's
Serenity Prayer: "God, grant me the serenity to accept the
things I cannot change, the courage to change the things I can,
and the wisdom to know the difference." Some versions
ascribed to his pupil Winnifred Wygal put courage first and

serenity second and that is probably the correct order. But for these purposes it is important to note what cannot be changed. And today, that is the weight and nastiness of criticism.

Or at least it can't be changed by you.

It is always a difficult decision as to how far to counter it directly. At one level you want to correct something which is untrue or unfair. On another, you draw attention to the criticism by attacking it, and rebuttal takes time. It is possible you can be right and wrong at the same time.

I have concluded that in the end it's better to treat criticism like sharing a home, which you neither own nor can escape from, with a psychopath, who you are unable to remove. You are ever-mindful of his presence. At times—hopefully, as few as possible—you will have to drop what you're doing and concentrate on what he's up to. But once you accept that he won't leave and you can't escape, you find a way to go about your business, knowing that he may be part of your life but that he is not going to define it.

Now you may say, and many do: what the hell! I don't choose to enter this house at all. Let someone else live with the psychopath. Unfortunately, the house and its unwelcome occupant come with the territory. And the business you want to conduct, which means a lot to you, which bestows purpose in your life, can only be done from that home with that companion in residence.

So, you accept the unavoidable. You construct your mental defences. You discipline yourself not to keep barging into his room to find out what he's doing or saying.

If you come across something unpleasant or cruel that has been written about you: DON'T READ IT! If it's a horrible headline, ignore it. If it's an awful article, don't look at it. And if you're unwise enough to peruse it, don't glance at the "comments" that follow!

None of this means that you shouldn't listen to sensible and serious criticism. You should. You can learn from it. But you won't learn anything from the stuff that's vomiting forth, that's written for clicks, that delights in its nastiness, that takes pleasure in the hope it is inflicting pain. And if you let it get to you, then you have lost, and "they"—whoever at any given time "they" may be—have won.

Treat the handling of criticism not as about the receiving of a blow, but as the willingness to be knocked down by it. See refusal and defiance as victories. Because they are.

And understand one thing, which I say constantly to the Leaders I work with and say often to myself: it matters less than you think. It defines you less than you fear. And, despite its vehemence, it lasts a shorter time than you thought possible. Remember, too, that the type of person who says or writes hurtful things, or who makes outsize claims or devotes energy to the expression of hate, has a problem less with you than with themselves.

In the end, however you choose to rationalise it, you do have to rationalise it, because otherwise you will lose effectiveness as a Leader. You will start to obsess about the criticism you receive, worry about it even though you know you shouldn't, and you'll despise yourself for letting it get to you. Absolutely nothing good can come of being drawn into its grasp.

I know it's not easy. I went from being enormously popular to being—according to all my critics and a few of my friends—very unpopular. It wasn't a great trajectory. But I knew that every moment I spent thinking or worrying about it would be a wasted moment.

I am tempted to resort to the cliché about "the price of fame." Like many clichés it is essentially true (which is why it became a cliché). Today that price is higher than ever for anyone in the public eye, from politicians to artists. Even those whose sole ambition and purpose in life is to become a celebrity all too often find that the initial warm glow of fame turns into a furnace.

So, if criticism distresses you, make a judgement about your capacity to cope with it. And if you think you can't, don't put yourself in a métier where it is inevitable.

By the same token, recognise that if what you're doing really matters to you and is something you're passionate about, you mustn't let the criticism or the anxiety it gives rise to stop you from pursuit of the thing you care about.

Realise, too, that judgements change, perspectives alter and that what seems anchored in the thickest of seabeds, time, circumstance and even serendipity can dislodge and bring to a different resting place.

So, this challenge for a Leader has to be faced. Think of it as a knotty problem you are obliged to solve. Objectivise it. Come to an understanding about it.

Otherwise, that psychopath will find you wandering aimlessly around the house, fretting, will sense weakness and will destroy you.

CHAPTER TWENTY-NINE

Scandal

All governments suffer scandals of one sort or another. In a dictatorship, they can be covered up—usually. In a democracy, as they gain traction, they can eat up huge amounts of energy, distract and distort the agenda of government, and leave the Leader frustrated and drained.

It's important to make a distinction here. Yes, scandals can arise that are the genuine article: scandals that uncover wrongdoing at the heart of the leadership, that put at risk the Leader and the whole government, and that can and often should result in their political demise. But for every one of those, there are fifty manufactured—at core trivial— or grossly exaggerated ones. They can't be ignored, since they have an impact on public opinion and the fortunes of the Leader; they have to be managed, but the Leader cannot afford to be obsessed with them.

When I was prime minister I lost count of scandals that fell into this second category. Some did have a germ of something in them. Some arose from misunderstandings that came to be represented as malfeasance. Some were literally confected out of nothing. All of them at the time consumed attention and focus that could have been directed more productively elsewhere.

And here's the thing. Once I left office, those scandals,

which had loomed so large when I was in power, faded; and what remained from my tenure as Leader were actual achievements or failures. In other words, the sense of perspective that had been so singularly lacking during the time scandal predominated curiously reasserted itself once I had departed. The experience is an important one to share, because it should encourage Leaders dealing with a scandal not to fall into the trap of becoming so obsessed with it that managing it obliterates the task of governing.

When you are in the eye of the storm—particularly when, as in Britain, the media is going into full attack mode—you believe the world is collapsing around you. Your obsession becomes even more pronounced if you consider the scandal more invented than real, because then a sense of injustice enters the mix.

But you have to remember that, provided what is facing you doesn't fall into the category of the full-blown, genuine, life-threatening scandal, it matters much less than you reckon it does. Of course, it will take its toll. You can't pretend it won't. But you need to remind yourself that just as the "scandal" itself is exaggerated, so you might be exaggerating its potential consequences, not least because the public care less, focus less, are interested less in what is going on in politics than you think.

Put another way: if, on an objective basis, the scandal isn't life-threatening, then it's unlikely to kill you.

That said, you still have to manage scandals when they arise. They come in all shapes and sizes. Often they involve ministers doing something wrong or stupid or both—financially, sexually, morally. Sometimes they are caused by misleading statements unintentionally made that then seem like "lies." On occasion they arise from the insensitive handling of a sensitive issue. They can be a tiny cloud on the horizon that without warning becomes a black sheet blocking the blue sky.

However they start, and whatever course they take, they will temporarily overwhelm the normal business of government and create a sense of crisis. They therefore demand the attention of the Leader.

While I was in office I learnt a number of lessons about managing scandals—generally by error.

First and foremost among these was the fundamental importance of establishing the facts before going into action. That seems obvious? Not really. A story appears. Maybe you don't fully appreciate its gravity. You speak before you know the facts and then learn too late that you have got them wrong. Now you're in full-scale and undignified retreat with, naturally, everyone assuming you knew all along. Before you utter a word, therefore, it's essential to get someone you trust to get you the facts. They may be the facts you prefer weren't the facts. But it's better to deal with the uncomfortable truth than pivot from a comfortable untruth.

The second lesson I learnt was that once I had established what was actually going on, I needed to decide the ground I was going to camp on. This is an important general lesson across a range of different challenges of government and almost deserves its own chapter. What it means in this context is that you need to work out your side of the story— your explanation, rebuttal, justification, whatever—in a way that you can hold to. That then becomes the ground you camp on.

All too often, Leaders, in their panic, choose the easiest or superficially most advantageous ground. This is fatal. It turns a scandal from one that can be managed into a new scandal about the original scandal, evoking the old cliché about the cover-up being worse than the deed being covered up.

A recent example in the UK is the scandal that came to be known as Partygate, involving an allegation that, contrary to the rules then in place to limit social contact during the Covid lockdown, those at the very centre of government in Downing Street were holding parties at which they mixed freely. Such a scandal would have been serious in any set of circumstances. It smelt of hypocrisy. A contempt of the governing elite for the governed. A sense of one rule for them, another rule for us. Certainly, a technical breach of the law. A long charge list. The way it was handled, though, turned it from a scandal to a crisis that threatened to bring down the prime minister, Boris Johnson.

Johnson failed to establish stable ground to camp on. Instead, he went straight out and flatly denied that any such parties had been held. Cue the inevitable production of large numbers of photographs showing people at Downing Street drinking together. Result: an even worse scandal as broken rules became accompanied by lies.

Holding parties and gatherings at Downing Street was certainly an extraordinary error of judgement. The rules at the time prohibited people mixing and congregating. They were a public health requirement for public protection, to limit the amount of social intercourse and so the spread of Covid.

What the staff in Downing Street were doing was technically illegal. They were, however, mixing together because they were fighting the virus and needed to stay at work. Whether they drank coffee or alcohol, were in the garden or in the Cabinet room or their office, made no difference. They were in each other's company by necessity. Yes, they were not following the same rules as the public, but this was inevitable. The rules for the public about parties were there to prevent people who weren't in contact with each other initiating that contact. It wasn't to do with the activity but the congregation. So, of course, adherence to the rules concerning parties for the general public would not have the same practical effect on spreading the disease as for those mandated to work together.

Had the prime minister admitted the parties, the fact they breached Covid rules, the error of judgement involved in allowing them, but explained the context, there would still have been a scandal for sure. But it would have been, though horrible, manageable rather than becoming job-threatening.

If it's essential to establish the best ground to camp on, it is advisable—when the scandal is complex or the facts unclear—to play for time. You need to make sure that everything is properly investigated internally before it's defended or dealt with externally.

Be careful, in playing for time, however, not always to default to holding an inquiry. Public inquiries have their place, especially when they deal with important subjects not being debated in the heat of contemporary politics. The 2010 Saville Inquiry into the 1972 shooting of twenty-six unarmed protesters by British soldiers in Derry on "Bloody Sunday," which was in essence part of the Northern Ireland peace process, is a good example.

But when the inquiry is one involving a hot political topic of real and sustained political controversy, and especially where it either is or becomes a full-blown statutory inquiry, tread very cautiously. Otherwise, a day's OK publicity for the announcement of the inquiry is then followed by months or more likely years of pain, without contributing much to the understanding of the topic under investigation.

The problem with an inquiry is that it can develop its own momentum, and the person conducting it, even if of a strong character, comes under intense pressure to find fault. Those in the media bluntly have no interest in a finding of innocence. They want someone to be found guilty. And if they sense that the person in charge of inquiring is wavering, they have ways of making them fall in line—their line.

Finally, as I learnt over time, never forget that the scandal is your problem, but it's not your job. Your job is governing, and people need to see that that is what you are focusing upon, and that—whatever controversies may be swirling around you—you're still out there talking about the things which matter to them. President Clinton did this brilliantly while he was going through his impeachment ordeal. Anyone else might have been consumed by the scandal, but he was still getting on with the job. No doubt a large part of his mind was occupied by it, but not the part of his mind the public was seeing.

One final, final point. Be mindful when in opposition of making too much of too little when it comes to scandal. It can be a boomerang, causing welcome damage on the way out, but inflicting harm on the thrower on the way back.

There will be scandal. Don't think for a moment there won't, no matter how squeaky clean you think you are. There is too much going on in government, too many actors involved in the performance, too much scrutiny from too many critical eyes to avoid it.

But keep it in its place.

CHAPTER THIRTY

Politics in the Era of
Social Media

We live in a new era of media. Conventional and social. And to be fair, it has its strong upside. Social media does give people the opportunity to communicate directly. It can be an antibiotic to poisonous material as well as spreading it. It does indeed offer a voice to communities which may live in political systems that don't allow independent voices. People use it. They do so because they like it. And for some, it has opened up new life possibilities and avenues of perfectly legitimate experience and adventure. This much is obvious.

However, to state something else obvious, it has its downside and, for sure, has completely altered the way political debate is conducted in ways which can be deeply destabilising and discomfiting for politicians. It is angry. Often unfair. Frequently misguided or misdirected. Inaccurate. Distorting. Both worthy of being ignored and impossible to ignore.

Social media has given birth to the era of the loudmouth. And while it's always been the case that those who shout loudest don't necessarily deserve to be heard most, when it comes to politics on social media platforms, shouting loudly seems to be the behaviour of choice for many.

I used to hold the naive view that social media might help to make conventional media more objective, by being an alternative for those searching for facts separated from commentary. Wow. Definitely got that wrong!

Precisely the opposite has occurred. Social media is itself highly partisan, with information, and judgements about what that information means, conflated, usually in a deliberately provocative way. At the same time, partly through social media, technology has created a wide diversification of the media but therefore also a much more competitive environment for the traditional news outlets.

The effect on conventional media has been to make it compete, compete on clicks, compete on outrage, compete on what catches your emotion rather than your reason. As this has happened, it has fragmented, seeing its commercial survival as dependent on garnering a constituency which is best retained by playing to already formed opinions and stirring them. The consequence is that a sharp grievance politics subsumes rational consideration of difficult choices.

Both social and conventional media then combine to create echo chambers of opinion, where instead of people learning about the other point of view, the view they had already is reinforced.

On social media, threads of political or other statements, even if based on one foundational fact which happens to be untrue, run riot.

The strength of an opinion is often in inverse proportion to the knowledge of the person holding it.

"The people have a voice" is a commonly expressed sentiment in favour of social media. Unfortunately, that means all the people, including the crazy ones. The people you might notice at the end of the bar droning away and could avoid, now pop up in your face.

Seeing things written there on screen has a curious effect. The people writing feel a sense of power; and the people reading it or who are the objects of it—often hateful stuff— feel that power irrespective of the validity/accuracy of what is written.

Conspiracy theories are one element. But in a way, those, even if annoying, are easily discounted. The conspiracy theorists are a niche group, and mostly a threat to themselves— though it is alarming to note how any theory, no matter how bonkers, can accumulate an audience which runs into the thousands and hundreds of thousands. If 1 per cent of the British population is off their head, it seems small as a percentage. But mathematically it's 650,000 people. Which rather changes the feel of it.

Much worse and more worrying, however, are the campaigns around issues led by opinion-formers who aren't inventing things but "one-siding" them. You take an international dispute and just present one side's version, usually heavily biased and distorted. That then, if followed by enough people, creates anger around the issue, makes compromise harder, inflames rather than informs.

Or there is the lambasting of statements people have made, by misrepresenting what they said or ignoring the context in which they have said it or giving one half of the statement and not the other, which results in imbalance.

Then, of course, there is the direct use of social media by foreign governments interfering with the internal politics of a country. This is now highly visible in Western democracies, where at least it can be exposed and therefore its impact somewhat limited, though there will at some point and not too far away be a necessity to examine how regulation might prevent or deter this practice. But it is hugely serious in places like the Sahel in Africa where campaigns of disinformation have helped destroy democratic government and engender hostility in local populations, particularly in respect of France as a former colonial power.

And to top it off, social media is a place where vitriol and venom are the sauce flavouring whatever opinion is being given vent to. Elected politicians are subject to degrees of unpleasantness, rudeness and verbal violence that are both shameful and unfortunately quite commonplace.

The cumulative effect is a background against which serious political debate, the exchange of views, the willingness to dispute without demonising, the pursuit of the right not the easy answer, becomes much tougher.

That's a rough world in which to try to argue for ideas, policies and plans.

And yet those characteristics of public discourse are important for a Leader trying to communicate with the people they serve.

Yes, it has its positive side. But overall, there will come a time when its effects are recognised as so consequential for political debate and democracy that it will need much more assertive regulation than currently exists.

In any event, it is a fact of political life and has to be mastered by a Leader in the modern age.

There are people much more expert than me to advise on

how to do it. My concern is rather to make sure the Leader recognises social media's power and its effect without getting mesmerised into thinking it alters the basic rules of politics, because it doesn't.

There are two things to remember about it. First, the public reads it, creates it, but also has an innate sense that the description I have just given of it is essentially true. Therefore, they buffet politicians with it, and at the same time want politicians to be strong enough to withstand it and treat it with the respect it deserves—which is often not much.

Never underestimate the degree to which people crave leadership. Back to Moses again. The Israelites simultaneously hated and craved his leadership. If you remember, they reached the promised land (though, yes, I know, he didn't).

In the social media world, strength as a political Leader, always important, becomes even more so. The worst the people can think of you as a Leader is that you are bullied— or bulliable, if there is such a word. Even some of those who agree with the criticism being made don't want to see you bend. The more ferocious the onslaught, the more the reward for staying upright.

Surf the wave of every passing current of Twitter opinion, and you may enjoy spasmodic popularity, but you will ultimately be disregarded as a Leader. People want a sense not that someone is indifferent to what social media is saying—it can be revealing an important truth—but that you as a Leader are prepared to be the rock on which the wave breaks, not be swept away by it.

The second point to bear in mind is that while social

media intensifies and complicates the business of communication, it doesn't alter its fundamentals. If anything, it makes them even more important. The narrative needs to be even stronger. The sense of purpose even more pervasive. The ability to fight your way through the garbage and pull out the gem even more critical.

Your response has to be that you become ever more savvy and capable. You don't circumvent social media. You utilise it. It is what it is. A pain. Super irritating. Enraging. But only you can decide the degree to which it is a distraction.

PART VII

You the Leader

CHAPTER THIRTY-ONE

Avoid Paranoia, Even Though They Are Out to Get You

You got there. You are the Leader. You won! Which means others didn't. Leadership breeds resentment with infallible impregnation. Rivals want your position. People who knew you when you were nothing may be happy if they like you, but will certainly be jealous if they don't. And as we have seen, since the Leader is on a continual fast-moving decision treadmill, any decisions taken will themselves create an almost unlimited potential for resentment, discord or even just plain old-fashioned principled opposition.

So, from the moment you reach the top of the pole, there are tribes of people trying to pull you down from it. It is natural. And accepting that it is natural is an important part of inhabiting the right zone of temperament when it comes to doing the job. Pulling you down may even be reasonable— though accepting that is obviously hard for any Leader. There comes a moment when it is right that you go. You have been there too long; lost your way in terms of the agenda; forfeited for some reason the support of the public; become a liability even if, once, you were a saviour.

Therefore, pretty much from the outset, they are, in a sense, out to get you. Sometimes wrongly; sometimes rightly.

And the chances are that you didn't get to be Leader without some form of struggle. Unsurprisingly, you want to stay there or at least choose the time of your departure. You're probably not the type of person who goes gently. That's not a quality you exhibited on the way up, and it's unlikely you develop it on the way down.

You want to survive for the usual mix of the principled and the personal. And so you have to deal with the contenders, the pretenders and the offenders.

All of the above leads to a high potential for paranoia. And that is emphatically bad. Bad for the government, bad for decision-making and ultimately bad for you. It seeps in, and then it drains you of focus and energy.

And it takes many forms. Stuff appears in the media. Someone has briefed something. It may be untrue, a distortion or just generally unhelpful. Who leaked it? Who briefed? Why? I see Leaders who spend hours trying to work it out. Their staff are just as bad. Was it one of us who did it? Who has been talking to whom? Which journalists have been seen with which official?

All that speculation is nearly always pointless. You don't know. You may suspect wrongly. It can be harmful, too: the very act of enquiry creates an atmosphere of suspicion. Choose your staff well, people you trust. That is the only sure way to avoid the irritating breaches. Moreover, speculation is a distraction: every moment you waste on worrying who is behind a disobliging story is a moment not spent on the real-life challenges directly in front of you.

Social media has, of course, taken all this to a new level. Here, conspiracy theories run amok. When you're the

Leader you become the target of them. Some of the conspiracies are said to be against you, and some initiated by you. It's a truly crazy world out there. But you can't let it all divert you or induce in you paranoia about why they're doing it or how you counter it. I am not saying you don't have to answer things that are being said and are untrue, but you need to do it quickly and then move on. You should not obsess about why it's happening, what's really behind it, who's really behind it.

Don't let your concerns and anxieties poison important working relationships. They should be maintained even if you believe that some of those you work with do indeed want your position and seek it. Acting contrary to the interests of the government or deliberately undermining the Leader is wrong; ambition for the top job is not. Learn to tell the difference. Or at least acknowledge there is a difference.

I had this conversation frequently when I was prime minister because—as is widely known—Gordon Brown, who was my Chancellor of the Exchequer and thus a vital cog in the government wheel, aspired to succeed me, and sooner rather than later. My folk understandably didn't like this. I used to say, he's entitled to want the job.

In my post-Downing Street years, I have spent a lot of time in the Middle East and in the Arab world, where wild stuff spreads across the media like a forest fire. I have seen Leaders become fixated by it. It's never helpful.

In general, politics is much more cock-up than conspiracy, but conspiracy is so much more exciting that it almost invariably takes over. I myself am constantly reading about plots that I'm supposed to be involved in to overturn particular regimes—as if I would have the means, let alone the inclination. There are dark theories as to intentions and motivations. I have so regularly been the subject of conspiracy theories, in fact, that I have just grown to live with them.

When I was prime minister, I had to deal with innumerable conspiracy theories arising out of the tragic death of Princess Diana. To this day, there are those who are convinced it was part of some nefarious Secret Service plot. It's all complete nonsense, of course; all driven by a paranoid belief that there has to be a deeply concealed reason for such a terrible and unexpected event.

The conspiracy theories about Princess Diana's death also exemplify the belief some people have in the existence of the deep state—a belief that generates a whole encyclopedia of paranoia of its own. Like so many of the worst paranoia creations, there's just enough truth to it to fuel it. In most countries, there are indeed institutions that over time develop views, attitudes and positions that become relatively embedded and remain constant through changes of government. The institutions act in accordance with those embedded principles unless redirected; and occasionally, if they feel very strongly about something, they will resist redirection. So, superficially, the government has one policy; but underneath, down deep, the system has another.

In democracies the deep state is highly constrained. In undemocratic countries, much less so. In both cases, Leaders should avoid exaggerated assumptions about the power such "hidden" forces have to thwart or to instigate.

In established democracies, in my experience, most

officials are averse to frustrating deliberately the work of an elected government—or doing anything the media, which adores a conspiracy, might find occasion to sink its teeth into. Their greatest anxiety—and this is true even, and sometimes especially, of those in such institutions as the intelligence services—is that they will get caught up in some political shenanigans and then be summoned in front of inquiries, committees and commissions and be criticised.

There will be occasions where "the system" will conceal or close ranks around a difficulty or a scandal. But that is usually in pursuance of a mistaken desire for self-preservation rather than some malevolent hidden hand trying to destroy legitimate government.

Some nations—Pakistan, for example—do have a deep state that can pose genuine problems for a democratically elected Leader; and developing countries on the whole have a larger challenge than developed ones. But even here, not everything is the product of deep state policy, and where it is and where it is contrary to the policy of the democratically elected government, it can be confronted and changed. As for countries that are not democracies, the chances are it's the Leader who is controlling the state, not the state the Leader.

If the paranoia induced by fear of a conspiracy is corrosive, so is the influence of the "whisperers" who surround the Leader. These may be staff, colleagues in government, friends, or just those wanting to exhibit some special knowledge. They may be people who love to be bearers of tittle-tattle dressed up as news, or conveyors of things the Leader "really should know." Some genuinely want to protect, some are looking to prove their utility or hoping to gain an advantage. All should be avoided. They sow the seeds of doubt and thus of paranoia.

How many times must it be stressed that Leaders are human? We all listen to gossip. We all incline an ear to someone telling us something that concerns us, especially if it is something that plays on our fears and stimulates our inner insecurities. How many times must it be repeated that an ability to resist such tendencies is an integral part of leadership?

Watch the whisperers. They're lethal.

Having said all that, one final point should be made, or any Leader reading this will think my advice hopelessly naive (and naivety is definitely not sensible in politics). Sometimes it becomes clear there really is a plot and they really are out to get you!

If that's the case, then act. Sort it—ruthlessly, if necessary.

The rest of the time don't imagine it, don't spend valuable governing time searching for it, and as ever in leadership, deal with it with cool detachment.

CHAPTER THIRTY-TWO

The Hinterland

Emotionally, leadership is a bundle of contradictions. Leadership is lonely. Leadership is voluntary. It is an extraordinarily tough job to be Leader. You fought hard to get the job. You have power. You have responsibility. You may exult in the one, and be intimidated by the other. You may want everyone to be your friend. Yet you know you are going to make many enemies. You're famous, but also infamous. You're a celebrity and people want to take photos and selfies with you but, unlike other celebrities, you're also a decision-maker over their lives.

You're liked and resented in varying proportions, and that mirrors in a way what you feel about being Leader. You like the power and the ability therefore to change things. But you resent how your motives are sometimes misconstrued, and you are frustrated by your incapacity to please the people when you're trying to do your best for them.

There is excitement; on good days fulfilment. But there is stress; and the days of frustration and disappointment are frequent. And all the time the relentless spotlight is casting its beam not only on your job, but on your life, your character, your family, your friends. The people who are unforgiving of your mistakes and who delight more in your failure than your success. Those who are careless of the consequences on you as a person, because in the role of Leader, you cease in a sense to be a human, you're a power, unreachable by ordinary people and therefore, because of the entitlement which power gives you, disentitled to sympathy.

But as my wife always said to me when I complained— usually about some media barb or attack—"No one makes you do it; if you don't like it, you can leave; and if you're not leaving we have to assume you like it more than you hate it."

When you reflect on the awesome nature of the responsibility, you do, or at least I did, shudder a little. It weighs on you mightily, and frankly, if it doesn't, you shouldn't be there.

The pressure and stress are real. To survive you have to create a coping mechanism. Some of it comes from possessing the right temperament, a very important quality in leadership: the ability to rise above, to keep calm when the situation is the opposite of calm, to have that little touch of Zen, that exuding of confidence externally, whatever the battering tremors roiling your insides. Such a temperament is vital because, apart from anything else, if the Leader starts to look panicky, the team and system collapse, shredding discipline and efficacy as they do so.

I was incredibly lucky in my core team—exceptionally talented and exceptionally brave. At moments of crisis, they would stand up when others would sit back, march towards the gunfire, and take an almost perverse pleasure in doing so. But even with that team, who knew me well and were at the top of their game, I knew as Leader I had to have my best face on, whatever might lurk unseen behind it.

A resilient temperament is a natural gift. And some have more of it than others.

But a hinterland can support it, replenish it, even grow it.

It was Denis Healey, the Labour Chancellor of the Exchequer in the 1970s, or it may have been his indomitable life partner Edna, who described the secret of his success in politics as having a "hinterland." By this, he meant having dimensions to your life which were not about politics, but about culture, art, a hobby, a passion nothing to do with political ambition; a place, mentally or physically, of rest, relaxation, leisure or pleasure. For Denis, it was poetry, music and, in later times, farming.

When I was prime minister, I played the guitar, even if only for a few moments, virtually every day. I would read, always with two books on the go, usually one about history, and the other maybe a thriller. I would watch movies, particularly the classics. I would try to learn about something of which I was ignorant: art, painting and pottery, or science— one of my deepest life regrets being that I never studied science properly at school and have ever since felt the absence of basic scientific knowledge a disadvantage.

Friends are important. Real friends. Preferably those you knew before you were ever anybody: friends from school, university, from when your kids were young. Of course, even with those, you never escape political discussion and they can't help but be interested in what you're doing. But you feel confidence in their company. You know you can be off guard, without risk. There is trust. With your political friends, however close, it's not that you don't trust them, but that they're mixing in other highly political and media circles and that they cannot but reflect something of what you're saying to them in what they're saying to others. So, the risk of indiscretion is there, even if unintentional.

The "friends" you have to be very cautious about are those who arrive as you arrive in power. One of the most important lessons I learnt as a Leader is that you mustn't fool yourself when you're apparently surrounded by people being respectful to you, deferential even, who tell you how remarkable you are, who appear to be supportive of your every move, professing their loyalty and your under-appreciated genius, seeming to embrace you when they are really embracing your power.

Don't be so cautious you overlook the ones who will still be there years later—and I have had a few. But be realistic enough to know that most are there for self-interest. Not an unconscionable reason, but one which should make you wary.

This can happen with people from outside politics and the system; and it can happen with people within it. I lost count of the number of ministers who, after I made them ex-ministers, discovered not just what an awful Leader but person I was, when I promise you as ministers they would marvel openly at my brilliance and integrity. There were civil servants who I genuinely thought admired and liked me, who, it turned out, invariably after I relinquished power, in fact thought I was an unprincipled airhead.

You could become somewhat jaundiced about human nature because of such people if it weren't for the others, the decent ones, who said what they meant, meant what they said, and would stand by you even when the going was horrible.

So, friends are an important part of the hinterland, but choose them carefully and realise the newer they are the more care should be exercised.

And then, naturally, there is the family. I found having teenage children with me in Downing Street an absolute blessing. Teenage children are of course commonly a nightmare. We had our share of those (but good news, parents currently of teenagers, they improve!), with sometimes quite high-profile consequences. And at the end of a highly disturbing and difficult day, you would be forgiven for thinking that the last thing you need is a showdown with a bolshy sixteen-year-old. You would be right, except that the absorbing effect of the showdown curiously displaces the stress of the "torrid day at the office."

Your family is the heart of your hinterland, and you have to make time for them and, most of all, leave some emotional energy for what matters to them. I can say this is exceptionally important because, to my deep regret, I so often failed to do it. But I never regretted or resented the time or energy I did spend, even if it was just sitting down and watching some crazy cartoon with five-year-old Leo. As it happened, and mostly due to Cherie and our helper Jackie, the children turned out fine. But you should never take a risk with family; it is never worth it.

This hinterland of hobbies, interests, friends and family helps you cope. It relieves some of the stress. It keeps your feet on the ground.

But there is a final reason it matters, and it's quite a selfish one: it makes you a better Leader, not only because you're less strung out and exhausted but because, thanks to that, you think more clearly. It normalises you in an environment which is acutely abnormal. You see dimensions that otherwise, immersed in the business of governing, you would be blind to. It gives you feel and touch, and all those invisible and intangible elements which add up to well-grounded instinct.

Make sure your schedule has time for the hinterland. Have some evenings in the month when you have dinner with people you really want to dine with, where you can relax and, within limits, let your hair down; make some of the weekend like the weekends other people have; be present with your family even if you're somewhat distracted. You can do it!

If the person running your diary cannot provide such moments, get someone else who can.

And if, in the years of climbing to the top, you haven't managed to create a hinterland, do so. It will make you a better Leader of the land you govern.

CHAPTER THIRTY-THREE

Hubris and Nemesis

The word "hubris" has a bad connotation. Its origins lie in Greek mythology, where it describes those who, though human, believe they are better than gods or, even if gods, show excessive pride or abuse their power. Their arrogance leads to their downfall. Nemesis is the divine retribution for such sinful behaviour that brings about the downfall.

As the Bible has it: "Pride goeth before a fall." Typically, the British have one word—pride—with two meanings: pride that is arrogance; and pride that is delight in an achievement or in a job well done. The French—more precise—have two words: *orgueil*, which is pride of the sinful sort; and *fierté*, which is pride of the good sort.

I will sometimes sit with Leaders who are riding high in the polls, the political sun is shining, they're basking in approval, and, perfectly naturally, they're exuding confidence and an air of general invincibility.

I almost want to grab them by the shoulders and shout: "Beware! Nemesis is right behind you!"

I don't, of course. I just say: "Well, that's great, but it may not last, you know."

Because, usually, it doesn't. I meet them some time later. The brow is furrowed, the complexion is a few shades more pale and the voice which seemed so strong is a little more quavering.

Nemesis has come in the shape of a crisis, an event, an unforeseen reversal in one form or another, and suddenly the sun is no longer shining.

And, again—usually and in retrospect—the reversal should have been predicted. But hubris prevented it.

Not always. President Jokowi in Indonesia, for example, was more popular at the end of his time than the beginning. But I promise you he's the exception!

When things are going really well, that's the time to worry about what could go really wrong.

Hubris, in its most egregious form, combines overbearing arrogance with malevolence.

But hubris can also stem as much from ignorance as vice. Here the sin lies in the characteristics described in the next chapter—thinking you know more than you do; a belief that you have the power to affect a situation that you can't, or at least not in the way you want; an overly exuberant conviction that you can overcome the odds, however much they may be against you; a faith that by sheer force of conviction you can triumph over an embedded reality.

Sometimes hubris arises from an unpreparedness for the unexpected. Things seem to be going so well that you don't spot the first tremors of upheaval. You're not seeing because you're not looking.

I have learnt over time and by my own mistakes that you should covet a healthy respect for what can go wrong and an equally healthy disrespect for your own or anyone else's infallibility. This sentiment of constant anticipation shouldn't lead to paralysis, but it should lead to circumspection. Because the fact is that the moment hubris takes a grip—even in its most benign form—nemesis is girding up her loins.

I could give numerous examples from my own time in government. I will declare two.

In the year 2000, with a strong lead in the polls, a weak opposition and a happy set of economic statistics, I failed to spot a gathering crisis resulting from an increase in fuel costs caused by a soaring oil price. A random protest blocking the delivery of fuel from what turned out to be an extraordinarily vulnerable and small number of fuel depots on which the country's petrol supply depended, quickly spiralled into a full-scale nationwide blockade. Within days the nation was grinding to a halt. Very bad.

At the same time, and completely unconnected, because inflation was low (a good thing) and pensions were linked to inflation (in principle, a sensible policy) we announced a risibly small pension increase. Resulting in very upset pensioners.

The two issues came together in a burst of disaffection at the government. The political scene became deeply fraught. We dropped 10 points in the polls. The opposition drew ahead for the only time in that parliamentary term. And what had seemed uninterrupted sunny weather just a few days before turned into a very nasty thunderstorm.

I had not made the connections I should have made and so not taken preventive action. A lesson learnt.

Much more serious was the aftermath of the terrorist attacks of 9/11. Putting aside for these purposes the rights or wrongs of removing the Taliban in Afghanistan and Saddam Hussein in Iraq, the fundamental miscalculation was to believe that, by changing those regimes from ones of brutal dictatorship to ones of democracy—a perfectly laudable aim in principle—we could overcome the absence, in those countries, of proper institutions of government, and the presence of religious sectarianism and of external players with an interest in undermining progress.

This was not an example of hubris in the sense of disdain for others or a belief in the overweening capacity of Western leadership to effect change. It was a misplaced assessment that the world as it should be could be forged from the world as it is, and that democracy could be transplanted into a political body that was going to have multiple pressures to reject the organ.

The belief in the inherent superiority of a democratic system gave us an exaggerated view of how and where it could take root.

The rise and fall of the former leader of Myanmar, Aung San Suu Kyi, offers another example.

I was and remain an admirer. She is a brave woman, and the world, which correctly recognised her as a martyr when she was imprisoned for years by the country's ruling military junta, has been too hasty in condemning her for not standing up against the oppression of the minority Rohingya population in her country when, as her removal and fresh imprisonment shows, her room for manoeuvre was much smaller than the outside world could understand.

In the early days when she became—at least the titular—Leader of the country, we had several conversations. I tried to describe the challenge of governing, how hard it was to make change, how I felt that she needed to recruit the right people to help, and how she should beware all the pitfalls she was certain to encounter. Basically, I tried to persuade her that being the people's idol was totally different from governing them.

She was polite but resistant. "The people love me," she would say. "But I will have to manage the military." I would reply that the people's love didn't eliminate the need to deliver, and that part of managing the military was to create enough practical change, particularly in the economy and government services, that their ability to interfere would be constrained.

I used the example of Nelson Mandela. He, too, was an icon, but, despite his global status, he knew that the political transformation he had wrought needed to be followed by on-the-ground change in the daily lives of people. In other words, he possessed the humility to recognise the limits of what he had achieved. The fact that his hopes for his country have not been realised by his successors is not a reflection on his personal qualities or powers of perception. They reflect the size of the task he knew he faced.

Aung San Suu Kyi was unpersuaded. Probably, in any event, she would have been brought down; maybe any change would have made the military even more fearful of the permanent loss of power. We will never know.

But I think, had she focused more on delivery, and relied less on her undoubted charisma and the love the people had for her, had she been able to give a sense to the country that political change had liberated the possibility of practical improvement, she would have stood a better chance of thwarting the junta forces, and rallying international support.

Hubris can sometimes arise not through an excess of confidence but through an inner, though unacknowledged, lack of it. "We can do it ourselves" is a cry I often hear from some presidents. They are the ones who fail. Fortunately, there are plenty today who are completely open to outside help and, where it is offered, are more than happy to take it. They're the ones who succeed.

I recall a conversation with one president who faced a significant problem with Islamist terrorism in his country, and was struggling. I suggested he bring in the Americans or the British. No need to, he responded. We'll deal with it. I explained that, around the world, there were countries with huge experience of how you track, monitor, disrupt and eventually defeat these groups, all of whom have a similar modus operandi. We don't need people telling us how to handle our problems, he said defiantly.

His terrorism problem grew worse. Too late he appreciated that he needed external help and started to seek it. Today, terrorism in his country remains an ongoing battle. With the help he has now secured, he might ultimately win it. But the lost years have taken a toll on his nation's fortunes.

Once you realise that hubris is a pervasive danger for Leaders, and once you see that, if indulged, nemesis is not far behind, your risk sensors become stronger. Your eyes stay wide open. You listen to advice and weigh it. A belief in your invincibility is replaced by a belief in your vulnerability, and you relax into it, knowing your decision-making will be better.

I think this is true of life more generally. Since leaving office, I have observed a lot of business leaders. Some have risen and stayed there. Those are the ones who prepare for every eventuality, who try to see round every corner, knowing that behind each one that looks nice something nasty may be lurking. They are the leaders who think—to switch Greek analogies—that Icarus is an object lesson in what to avoid.

The others—well, they're the ones you read about, the ones with their wings singed, falling to earth.

CHAPTER THIRTY-FOUR

You Are Never as Knowledgeable or as Smart as You Think You Are

The problem with winning, especially in what is often the "winner takes all" world of politics, is that you think you're smarter than you are, or indeed than anyone is. I won. Ergo I am brilliant. Or, at least, better than anyone else.

Since leaving office, I have met a big swathe of the business community, including, for fundraising purposes, a significant number of billionaires. They are often people who have had a great idea, pulled off an amazing deal, invented something clever. They have become wealthy. Good for them. I have noticed, however, that in some that success has given them a sense of self-belief that makes them think they're not only good at the thing that made them rich, but smarter than anyone on other things.

The political world contains similar offenders. You win a great victory or manage to ascend somehow to the top of what the nineteenth-century Conservative prime minister Benjamin Disraeli called "the greasy pole." You conclude that you're a genius. You figured it all out. You came through. You beat the rest.

You forget that it isn't only about ability; it is also about circumstance, the door of opportunity opening in a timely manner, the poor quality of the opposition and, of course, luck. Yes, be proud of the win. But don't let it fool you into thinking you're smarter or more knowledgeable than you really are.

As I wrote in an earlier chapter, politics is the one profession in the world that puts someone into a position of extraordinary power and responsibility without requiring any prior experience or demonstration of capacity on their part.

Naturally, there is a process of selection. You will have demonstrated a certain track record in the business of politics that makes you a contender; your colleagues will have had a say. You're not literally plucked from the crowd. But you may—likely, will—have had no actual experience of governing.

What you have had experience of is winning. That will have involved making judgements, taking decisions, fighting the good fight. These are not easy to do, so your success will have given you a measure of confidence in your own capability that is probably justified. But the important thing to recognise—right from the outset—is the limitations of the proof of that capability. Winning power doesn't mean you know how to govern. Having taken correct decisions to get to power doesn't mean you're an infallible decision-maker when faced with the infinitely tougher challenge of governing a country.

A degree of humility isn't the natural posture of most politicians. But if you don't have it, you will soon learn it, or go under.

There is a vast expanse of things you know little about.

Focused on attaining the position, you will not have focused in the same way on all the dimensions of reality you will be confronted with as Leader in government.

So, start with just a simple appreciation of the need to learn, an attitude that is accepting of the wisdom of others, an openness to ways of thinking about problems that aren't as you thought while campaigning to win.

I have been surprised, shocked and more than occasionally appalled at how much I have learnt since leaving office.

"I've looked at life from both sides now"—as Joni Mitchell sang. I know infinitely more about the world, despite having been prime minister of a significant country for ten years, and I have been able to study without the stress and struggle of running a government.

I have tried to build and to develop businesses and organisations, not simply think about regulating them. It's a lot tougher than I thought.

I have met people from all walks of life across all cultures and creeds, far beyond my native shores.

I have read papers not just for information but for reflection.

And here's a truly extraordinary thing: I have kept maturing. I left office at fifty-four. Old enough, you might think. But no, the process doesn't stop.

When I discuss this subject with other "formers," they immediately nod.

So, what should this tell you?

It should drive home the point that you may think you're a genius because you have succeeded in winning power, but you will find out sooner or later that it's not true. Try for sooner.

And the more I know, the more I realise how little I know. This is why the preparations for venturing into politics and the time you spend in it, in opposition, or on the way up, matter so much. Because there will come a time when you understand the limitations of your knowledge; when you understand what Roy Jenkins, the great Home Secretary and Chancellor of the Labour governments of the 1960s and 70s, meant when, in response to my asking what he was thinking about when he appeared pensive as we sat together before doing a radio broadcast, he said he was "contemplating the vast expanses of my own ignorance." And Roy was very definitely not an ignorant man.

When you're the Leader, you're the "Decision-Maker." You will make the decision. That's your job. But it doesn't mean you're the best person to be making that decision. There may be someone far better qualified. It's just that they're not the Leader.

In other words, don't mistake the fact that you're the decision-maker for an assumption no one knows better. There is a difference between being smart and being powerful. A Leader will usually be treated with more respect than they deserve by those who exist by reason of their patronage. The good ones—a few—will speak up when they think you're talking nonsense. The others—the many—won't. Let them try and fool you; but don't fool yourself.

CHAPTER THIRTY-FIVE

It's Better to Be Respected than Loved, Feared or "Trusted"

This chapter heading will jar. Surely it is good to be loved as a Leader? Yes it is, and that most often happens when the Leader is an iconic figure who represents an idea, but it won't happen to a Leader in the process of making difficult change.

Being loved by the people is a wonderful thing, but it isn't the objective of governing. Making change which improves their lives materially—economically and socially—this is the purpose, and precisely because it involves altering the status quo and upsetting interests along the way, it is unlikely to be accompanied by love.

And surely it is not good to be feared? Sometimes it is good, when a Leader trying to do the right thing is confronted by those trying to stop him or her and they need deterring.

Great Leaders use fear sparingly, but they use it. Great powers use it, too. Most of the time this is deeply resented. But there is an interesting lesson I have learnt about American power. It is true that countries resent it; think it is often wielded hypocritically, inconsistently or in a way which is self-serving. Allies frequently feel ignored, or consulted for form but not in substance.

But over a long time in politics, I have concluded that what worries allies most is American absence, and that what emboldens bad actors most is a feeling that America has wandered off the field of play. And even though I don't like many of the uses to which China's power is put, I want its allies, which now include Russia and Iran, to fear it sufficiently to exercise restraint when China wishes it.

And so to the issue of trust. It must unquestionably be good to be trusted? Trust is such an essential element in leadership—encompassing the ability to take people with you, guiding them through the difficult change, preserving unity in the face of challenge.

Well, here, it all depends on what you mean by "trust." In politics, it is an elusive concept, and we need to define what we really mean by it.

At one level, no one "trusts" politicians. My thesaurus lists 139 synonyms for trust; and a huge number are to do with certainty, confidence, expectation, hope, as well as, of course, truth.

But nothing is very certain in politics. Hope and expectation always run vastly in advance of what realistically can be achieved. And truth? "What is truth?" Pontius Pilate is supposed to have asked of Jesus; and in politics it would be a good question to ask.

Facts are true, despite the contemporary and hopefully temporary indulgence that feelings are as important as facts and that the latter can be changed by the former.

But in politics people often confuse opinions with facts and hold them to be "true." "Immigration is ruining the country," says politician X. "At last someone is telling the truth," a significant proportion of the population may say. And they conclude that this politician can be "trusted," as opposed to all the wishy-washy careerist ones who tell you it's more nuanced than that and properly controlled immigration is a good thing, who point out the role it has played in American economic supremacy, or in the UK technology sector, or who argue that foreign nurses and doctors are vital to the National Health Service, or that without migrant workers the hotel and hospitality sectors in virtually any developed country would collapse.

Of course, these are arguments which don't lend themselves to slogans or one-liners. The very presence of nuance makes for the absence of trust because it appears to be unsatisfying, mealy-mouthed, wavering or uncertain.

In politics, the populists are regularly hailed as the ones to be trusted, the ones "speaking truth to power," the ones challenging "the elites," "telling it like it is," unafraid to break with conventional thinking.

But, in reality, what they're doing is telling you what you want to hear, what you want to believe, what lifts your expectation not through hard graft but hot air.

I always say the time to trust a politician most is when they're telling you what you least want to be told. If you think about it, that's obvious. Any fool can work out what you want to hear; they just have to make a cover version of your own thoughts. It's a Leader genuinely wanting to do the best for you who will tell you that what you want is either not possible or not what you need.

I have kept this book mercifully light on Brexit, and here leave aside the pros and cons of the decision.

You can make the case that, in the long term, it is in Britain's interests to have left; that we can strike out in a new direction; that the short-term pain is worth the long-term gain.

What you can't seriously argue is that when we break up the trading arrangements with the partners with whom we do half our trade, we won't suffer at least some immediate commercial loss. It would be weird if it were otherwise.

Or that when we leave our continent's political union, we won't lose political influence, at least with them.

Yet that is exactly what the Brexit proponents claimed.

And I bet those proponents—Boris Johnson, Nigel Farage and others—will have enjoyed higher levels of trust when the Brexit referendum was held in 2016 than David Cameron, George Osborne and other pro-Europeans, even though the arguments the latter were deploying—namely that Brexit would cause economic damage and loss of political weight in Europe—were manifestly correct and have been proved so.

The point was that many people wanted to believe what the Brexiteers were saying and therefore "trusted" them more.

Any political Leader making difficult decisions will quickly run into "trust" issues.

A government spending money? High levels of "trust." A government cutting spending? Poll their "trust" figures at such a moment and they will be negative. But believe me, no politician cuts public spending out of a desire to do it, but because, rightly or wrongly, they think it is necessary for the long-term health of the country.

"Trust" is not a trustworthy concept in politics unless applied with strict care.

In any case, the daily business of politics militates against being trusted. Sometimes you're prevaricating; sometimes you're changing your mind; sometimes you're holding back; sometimes your promises turn out not to be false but to be unrealisable for reasons good or bad; sometimes you're just having to manage colleagues or circumstances, and can appear shifty as a result.

Of course, sometimes the Leader is dishonest or corrupt. Then it's a different ball game.

I don't actually know a lot of "truly" dishonest politicians. However, I do know a lot who are considered that.

Take French politics, for example. France is a tough country to govern. It votes for presidents who promise to change things. Those presidents start to make change. The nation revolts. Their "trust" ratings plummet. It's completely illogical: their "trust" ratings should rise.

Or think of the courageous voices across the Sahel region of Africa exposing, rightly, the utter myth (pushed often by Russian-inspired social media campaigns) that what is holding those countries back is some modern form of French colonialism. The myth is highly popular, the opponents of it unpopular. The first group enjoy high levels of trust, the latter not.

During the Covid crisis, I lost count of the number of people who would say to me that they didn't "trust" the politicians imposing lockdowns or seeking to rush out "unsafe" vaccines.

Now, there are perfectly legitimate arguments about the

extent of the lockdowns and even some about vaccination. But why would a political Leader advocate lockdowns unless they truly believed they were necessary? Or vaccination?

Those Leaders might have been right—I happen to think they were—or they might have been wrong. But there is no doubt that they believed in the policy they were pursuing. To have conducted this debate on the basis of "trust" is without any logic at all.

The point is: if you set out to be "trusted" as a politician you will find, over time, that it is a tough accolade to maintain.

Trust is better sought as a consequence of respect; and respect is something a Leader can and should attain.

Trust in this sense is not about arguing over who is most "honest" or who tells the most "truth," but about whether the Leader can be "trusted" with the nation, trusted to make decisions in what they genuinely believe is in the national interest.

Deep down, people know that politics can be a difficult, even dirty, business; and deep down they accept this. Frankly, they would not want an "honest" naïf in charge of their affairs.

They want someone to deliver; someone who has the ambition and the competence to govern; someone they respect as a Leader, not necessarily as a private character.

They don't like being told about hard truth and choices. But they will follow Leaders.

And ultimately, even if the Leader is doing unpopular things, even if the volume of complaint appears to drown out the patient explanation of necessity, respect can still be retrieved. That is a precious political asset.

And that begets trust of a different but to my mind deeper sort, not because you like the Leader or like their policies, but because you know they're prepared to serve you with a service only true leadership can provide.

To return briefly to love and fear. I know Leaders who come, in time, to be loved because the effect of their policies, however tough to administer, has been recognised as beneficial. But they're usually Leaders in wartime, or ones who can govern for a long period and be around to reap the benefits they have sowed.

But for those operating in a democracy, in peacetime, with term limits, constitutional or practical, it's rare enough for me to struggle to think of an example. Sure, they can be loved by their adherents, their fan base, but loved by the country—hmm, I don't think so.

And as for fear, except in the narrow sense I alluded to at the beginning of this chapter, even dictatorships can't rule by fear alone. For a time, of course; and maybe North Korea is an exception; but, overall, eventually the people rebel.

Fear doesn't engender respect. Leadership does. So, don't try to be loved and avoid being feared except when strictly necessary; aim for respect. It's not as beautiful as love or as satisfying to your inner demons as fear, but it's the only thing worth really "trusting" in politics.

CHAPTER THIRTY-SIX

Ambition: Calculate Too Much, and You Miscalculate

There is nothing wrong with ambition; and no politician will rise far without it. I had a notion when I first became an MP that just staying a constituency MP, doing my best for my constituents, would be enough, so thrilled was I to be in the Mother of Parliaments. That lasted all of about ten minutes. The moment I saw what power was and what it could do, I wanted it.

I wanted it for the usual mix of motives: to change the world, to put principle into practice, to be respected and recognised as a person with power and to feel that power, to feel how it could shape my world around me as well as the world of others. And for any other moderately successful politician the motives are roughly the same—though not necessarily in the order I've just given them.

Politicians who boast about their honesty/integrity/attachment to truth and goodness, as opposed to those "other politicians," make the seasoned among us reach for the bucket, precisely because we know politics and politicians can't be like that, and for sound reasons as well as bad.

Don't get me wrong. All those virtues are important. But the plain fact is that there is too much of the business of politics that involves wheeling and dealing, intrigue and some ruthlessness to permit it to be conducted by paragons.

Inevitably, as an aspiring politician, you are drawn to creating alliances, sometimes quite factional ones. You have to judge which fights to pick, when to speak up and when to shut up. You have to measure constantly the space between tactical necessity and strategic objective. It's a maze, and some politicians get lost in it. Their ambition eclipses their principles; they oscillate between this route and that, never quite finding the point of entry or exit, and so usually end up nowhere.

Not all. Some with very high levels of intelligence or huge political skill are able to negotiate the maze, despite the lack of a consistent plan of action. And never discount the role Lady Luck plays.

But such politicians are the exception. I wish to analyse the rule.

Let's begin at the beginning. Before you're a Leader. You're interested in politics and want to make it your career.

Ambition is clearly going to be in the mix from the start, but your first consideration should be that politics is best treated as a vocation, not a career. In other words, if you don't feel the intense desire to do it, don't do it. There is far too much misery and risk in the game to be in it unless you really want to play. With passion.

You then need to prepare yourself. And the initial preparation has to be based on the understanding that politics can't be done well unless you know about the world beyond it. When I advise young people who are thinking about pursuing a full-time commitment to politics, I start by telling them: do not go from university to become a researcher to an MP, then get selected as an MP, then work your way through the ranks. You might become very proficient at the business of politics if you take that route, but your practical proficiency for your country will be severely constrained.

It's far better to learn about the real world before you enter the parallel one of politics. Gain experience of how normal people live, work and think. See how businesses or, for example, schools or hospitals and other public services are run; how people have to make decisions in positions of leadership, day in, day out; what really matters and what only appears to matter. If you can, see another part of the world, become familiar with a different culture and language. It will never be time wasted if it's time spent learning.

The knowledge you acquire may or may not be of practical use to you later, but the immersion in something different, the honing of sensitivity to the concerns of the vast majority who do not spend their time obsessing about politics, will shape your political character in ways that will make you a better servant and a more informed master.

The small number of years—just seven—that I spent as a lawyer in a completely non-political field of work was hugely beneficial to me when finally I did become an MP. I worked with people who didn't care and never asked what my politics were. I realised that most people don't spend their time thinking about politics, obsessing over this item or that in the daily news, wondering who's up and who's down in the political world. Rather, they are deeply focused on their business, or their job, or the prospects for their family.

It gave me an acute sense of the "normal." And the distance between it and politics.

So, if you hanker after a life within politics, start with collecting as much knowledge as you can of the world outside it. That will make your ambition much more likely to result in fulfilment.

After that, if you wish to navigate the maze successfully, realise that belief—a set of convictions you hold sincerely and not just conveniently—is a vital accompaniment to that success.

Calculate too much and you miscalculate.

This may appear naive advice. But it is my personal experience. Two examples from my own political life prove my point. The first dates back more than forty years to when I was seeking to be selected as a Labour candidate in the 1983 election. I approached at least twelve different constituencies in the hope of being chosen by one of them. All rejected me, sometimes in favour of a would-be who, frankly, was barely sentient. It was depressing. It was also fairly readily explicable: I was avowedly and openly in favour of expelling the far-left Militant Tendency from the Labour Party at a time when to be against expulsion was a litmus test of leftist respectability. I would be doing well; that question would be asked and answered; and down my ship would go.

Just before the election, the constituency of Sedgefield— then a safe Labour seat and with a membership that was strongly anti-Militant—came up. Now a stance that had ruled me out in a dozen other constituencies became an advantage. I won.

And here's the thing: several of the seats for whose candidature I contested unsuccessfully ended up, because of the scale of Labour's 1983 defeat, being lost. Had I prevailed in the selection process for any of those, I would not have been in Parliament after 1983; and therefore, would never have gained the leadership eleven years later. In the end, sticking to my convictions paid off.

I became Leader of the Labour Party in much the same manner. After we had suffered our fourth election defeat in a row in 1992, I had become an out-and-out Labour moderniser, saying things much of the party found too bold or unacceptable. The then Leader, John Smith, even warned me good-naturedly to be less vociferous, because in his view it meant I could never become Leader. But I thought: what the hell, I'm fed up with perpetual opposition; I have a clear view of what is holding us back, and I am just going to say what I think—carefully but nonetheless plainly.

Tragically, John died. The leadership was suddenly vacant. The party decided it, too, had had enough of impotence in opposition and I became the exemplar of the old adage about right person, right place, right time.

I have seen the same thing happen many times with many of the Leaders I work with. The best ones. The ones who manage to stay the course. Sure, they will have played the game with skill, worked the corridors, done the glad-handing and occasionally backhanding. Lots of calculation will have gone into the mix, certainly. But at a crucial point, they stopped calculating and stood up.

Leaders take risks—sometimes the ones others won't or don't take. Emmanuel Macron would not have become Leader of France otherwise. Nelson Mandela wouldn't have become a political icon. Mikhail Gorbachev wouldn't have set in train the disintegration of the old Soviet Union which led to the liberation of Eastern Europe. Winston Churchill would not have led Britain through the war, or Charles de Gaulle France after it. All these Leaders, at some point in their career, took a stand that mere calculation in furtherance of mere ambition would have said was ill-judged.

This is not to say that those who strike strong positions and stick with them are necessarily people you may agree with. Margaret Thatcher has her detractors, of course, as well as admirers. But no one can seriously doubt that she stuck to what she believed in.

The new wave of populists in part succeed because people think they stand out against the prevailing wisdom, the soggy centre, the status quo. Now, this may be sham to the degree that some are populists absolutely through calculation. They take a grievance and exploit it, calculating that by doing so they gain political traction. But they will quickly be found out once they attain power, unless they have thought through their positions and have a plan and not just a performance.

So, this is not a plea to recognise how the "good guys" have principles and the "bad guys" don't. It's just a practical life lesson in political leadership. If everything for you is just a career calculation, understand the risk that the world changes and you're left with a miscalculation.

The one thing you can guarantee in politics is that what

seems immutable, one day becomes mutable: things often turn out unexpectedly. The politics can change. The circumstances can change. What was once apparent to you and a minority now becomes apparent to the generality of people. You have taken an unpopular stand on an issue, and your analysis has been proved correct. In a moment, what looked a foolish bet suddenly reappears as far-sightedness.

And "the people" will ultimately spot those who are believers and those who aren't. Again, to be clear, this doesn't make your beliefs right, it simply emphasises the point about what today we call "authenticity."

Ultimately, there is a deeper reason: politics isn't worth it unless you are genuinely acting according to belief. OK, power is power; and it's attractive, even a drug, which, once addicted to, is painful to give up. But unless you're an emotional robot—and I accept there are quite a few of those in politics—there is such a thing as peace of mind. You want to think you tried to do good, and even if you failed trying, you tried and failed for good motives.

There is a karma in politics and it has—as karma does— a way of reinstating itself, in the end. And for all politics and politicians, there is an end.

CHAPTER THIRTY-SEVEN

Don't Make Enemies Deliberately; You Will Make Enough Accidentally

The Leader has status, authority, power. They can appoint, anoint and annul. They will be surrounded by people wanting to please them, hoping to earn or achieve advancement, usually by any means possible. Such people may advance through merit. That's a full tick. Best in class. But if they can't do so through merit, they will seek to advance through flattery, through catching the ear of the Leader, through becoming apparently indispensable, through uber loyalty, through whatever tricks and twists work.

The Leader must be able to spot merit and reward it. They must also be able to manage those who lack it, but whose ambitions are nonetheless every bit as great as—sometimes greater than—those with it. This latter group can easily turn from being uber loyal to being uber disloyal, should their pretensions to advancement be thwarted or go unrecognised. And the unfortunate reality is that they're usually also the larger group, because real merit—stand-out talent—is rare in politics.

Such people, once they're not promoted as they believe they should be—or, worse, when necessity demands their demotion—swiftly become a potential danger. They realise that the Leader is no longer their route to advancement. They therefore gravitate towards others—and there are always others—who are willing to promise to deliver what the Leader has decided not to. They cease to be friendly allies and become hostile critics.

And that's not the only way that political enemies are made.

Some people like to bask in the reflected glow of the Leader, to know they count, to be able to say to their friends that they're friends with the Leader. They will be people of varying levels of influence, not ministers but invariably individuals with an acute sense of their own importance. They are very easy to slight. They are quickly offended if you forget things they think you should remember or fail to pay attention to them when they believe they deserve it. The smallest perceived lapse on your part will lead them to conclude that they have gone from preference to indifference in your eyes.

Moments of apparent neglect on your part are generally perceived rather than deliberate. Being Leader is a big task, devouring your energy and focus. It's unreasonable to expect that you should be alert at all times to what, compared with the size of the issues you're dealing with, are trivial matters. But the point is they're not trivial to those you are neglecting. It is ridiculous, infuriating and irrational that people unintentionally slighted should harbour resentment. But they do.

Then there are those who are jealous. Jealousy is a simple emotion, and we all possess the capacity for it. We try to conquer it, but it is an insidious and clever manipulator of our psyche and knows how to present itself as something different and more principled. Leaders shouldn't kid themselves on this front. However nice people are to their face, they are essentially living in a habitat awash with tiny invisible goblins of jealousy, waiting for Leaders to stumble or if the opportunity arises tripping them up.

All these categories of folk can tip very easily from mild dislike to active hostility. Even at their most positive, they're only a pinprick away from being enemies.

Then, of course, you get those who are opposed to you because they genuinely disagree with you. Yes, there are such people! Their disagreement may be cordial, but it can just as easily turn nasty. It may well be principled, but in politics the political and the personal are hard to distinguish.

The point is: you will make enemies, lots of them, legions of them, and you will make them unintentionally, occasionally not even noticing that you have done so. It follows, therefore, that you shouldn't make enemies deliberately, because you will make enough of them accidentally.

Act at all times with good grace. My dad taught me at an early age that charm costs you nothing. Smile and be pleasant. It's not difficult. Kindness is a virtue which is available to anyone. Exhibiting it won't stop you accumulating enemies, but it will at least enable you to minimise them and, for the objective observers of your world, persuade them that the enmity is unjustified or exaggerated. It all helps.

By the same token, a Leader should never bear a grudge. Grudges are wasted energy. They are pointless and mentally time-consuming. They are bad for the esteem in which others hold you and in which you hold yourself. They're also a sure way of converting someone who dislikes you into someone who hates you.

Of course, a Leader should both display and demand loyalty. And those who are disloyal should be removed for the good of the entire project. That is good leadership. Incompetence should also have consequences. Tolerating it is a leadership failure. The Leader who fails to take such steps as are necessary, who shows weakness or who—maybe out of friendship or fear—permits the disloyal and incompetent to remain part of the team, sends a bad message across the organisation, demoralising those who are loyal and competent, and creating an environment in which poor behaviour is seen as indulged.

But being firm over bad behaviour is completely different from bearing a grudge because of it. Settling a score—using one's power, authority and status to inflict injury on someone for no discernible governing purpose other than that they deserve it—is wrong. Such an action is an extension of ego, not an expression of leadership.

Leadership is best exercised when the senses are cold, not hot; calm, not stormy; detached from personal rancour; when the teeth are not grinding or gnashing and the eyes are seeing the whole picture, not the small corner to which they are drawn by irritation or anger.

And there's another reason why it's a mistake to be too quick to burn bridges. While it's true that in politics your friends can become enemies, it's also the case that your enemies can become, if not friends, at least colleagues.

When as prime minister I was considering appointing or promoting someone, those close to me would sometimes say: "But have you seen what they once said about you?" I would respond: "I don't care; they're of use now." People fall out with you, but you should always be prepared to let them fall back in.

Maybe you had a real and profound disagreement over an item of policy. Don't treat it as personal. Perhaps in the future another item will arise over which you find yourselves in agreement and for which you need their support. Don't make it impossible for them to give it.

The word "ruthless" literally means without pity. But in the political context, it is better understood as meaning without discolouring emotion. There is nothing wrong with emotion—we're human. But emotion should not discolour. It should not warp. When a Leader acts ruthlessly, the absence of pity is because of the presence of purpose. In this case, being "ruthless" is a strength. But being without pity out of resentment, this is weakness dressed up as strength. And it rarely fails to bring misfortune.

In those political systems that operate according to a proportional voting system, coalitions are the usual order of things. And they shift constantly. I have watched governments, in such systems, being formed of coalitions between wildly varying parties, some of whom have seemed viscerally opposed to each other, yet who somehow found the ability to come together when necessary.

But such cooperation is always harder when the opposition is visceral not in a political sense but a personal one. Then you're not simply negotiating over different policy positions but overcoming emotional angst and fury. That's much tougher.

So, remember: your job is to lead. There is no space for anything which saps your energy or attention or is not substantially important for governing.

CHAPTER THIRTY-EIGHT

Create a Constituency, Not a Clique

I like the elevated parts of politics—the ideas, the policy formation, the decision-making, the challenge of meeting a problem, wrestling with it and solving it. These are the things that stir my blood, activate my senses, give me the feeling the whole business is worth the frequency of pain and disappointment.

But these on their own are not sufficient for survival in the uniquely hazardous street life of politics' inner city, where the gangs roam, every corner has its own assassin lying in wait, even the most harmless-seeming passer-by can suddenly turn feral, and ambition and intrigue cohabit in deadly combination. You need people around you who will support, protect and fight for you, who will form a circle around you and provide an iron shield as you walk the street. In other words, you need a constituency—a party, a movement, a group or cadres, foot soldiers.

I learnt the importance of this dimension of leadership the hard way—through being bad at it. By the end of my time in office, I had a group of people around me who supported my ideas and policy direction and who were indeed courageous and willing to stand up, fight and protect. But there weren't enough of them and they weren't organised in the way I needed.

Because party management frankly bored me, I too often neglected it. That was a mistake. And not one to be proud of. On the contrary, failing in this dimension involved a failure to lead. It was an act of incompetence, because competence in this area is a crucial part of leading well. It wasn't that I didn't have people—close aides—doing a lot of the hard work in the party and doing it with great skill. It was that I failed to appreciate that, at a certain point, they could not substitute for me. They could help carry the burden, but I needed to be at the centre of the carriage.

Engagement, then—with a political party in the conventional sense, or a movement or even a faction within a broader base—is crucial for a Leader. While you're in opposition, this is relatively easy. Though it may not seem so then, you have more time on your hands than when you're in government. And, in one sense, party management in opposition is your equivalent to governing. Managing the party well shows your executive ability. This matters, because it is evidence of a capability to govern, even though the significance of the decisions taken is obviously much smaller.

The key to successful leadership is to continue with this management in government when the pressures are all countervailing. Now you don't have the time, the energy, even the patience to worry about the party because you're weighed down with decision-making that affects real lives with real consequences. But you have to find that time, energy and patience, because managing your constituency will better enable you to make those decisions in the manner you want.

Disgruntled foot soldiers don't make for a well-performing army. So, don't regard as an intrusion time and energy spent keeping your cadres gruntled. Regard it as a professional necessity. Remember that for those working on your behalf, down in the bowels of the body politic, you as Leader quickly become a remote figure. They may admire you, but they need to know that you admire them, regard them as essential, see them as vital to the health of that body.

Remember, too, that these foot soldiers fall into two camps: those who are presently foot soldiers but have a natural and often well-founded ambition eventually to be officers or even leaders; and those who are content as foot soldiers and who either have the self-awareness to know that is the limit of their capacity or have chosen to limit themselves and have no larger ambition. The first group need to know that there is a route of advancement and that you as Leader appreciate it is your duty to help them advance. The second group need to know that you appreciate their importance, that they're not beneath you but alongside you, that you do not take them for granted or confuse their lack of ambition with a lack of pride or desire for acknowledgement.

Your engagement with these groups needs to go beyond occasionally turning up and making a speech. The schedule—that indispensable prop—has to create space for meetings that allow for dialogue, opportunities to explain, the sharing of arguments they can use with opponents of your policy, to educate, to cultivate and to generate support. The personal things—marriage, children, deaths in the family, achievements outside the political arena—should also be noted and celebrated. The foot soldiers need to be inspired by your purpose and leadership, but they also need to feel they're part of it—integral, indeed. Each may be a cog in the wheel but they're a cog without which the wheel doesn't turn.

In the first flush of victory when you sweep to power, all this may appear redundant, a nice to do but not a primal duty. But when the tough times come—and inevitably they do—the importance of this constituency will become manifest. That's the moment when you'd better find it's ready to be mobilised rather than suddenly discover you need it.

And don't mistake a clique for a constituency. Of course, any Leader will have an inner circle of close allies. These are partners in the whole endeavour, those with whom you share intimate political thinking, anxieties and secrets. They're the people you enjoy spending time with, because the trust is there that allows indiscreet musing among the illuminati, in a métier in which, as a general rule, musing is unwise and indiscretion severely punished.

But that's not at all the same thing as a constituency: not in scale, and not in why and how it is brought into being and maintained. The clique provides comfort. The constituency provides protection. The first makes your life more bearable. The second keeps you alive.

Unfortunately, and occasionally disagreeably, your constituency's needs can go beyond simply feeling your love. They need sustenance of a more tangible kind. This could take the form of a policy position that really matters to them; a move symbolic or substantial that proves you're one of them. If it matters to you too, that's fine, naturally. But if it doesn't or, worse, runs counter to your thinking, you need to weigh things up very carefully. It's possible you may have to concede on something for a lower purpose in order to achieve an overall higher purpose. There is, in my view, nothing unprincipled about doing this.

Of course, if it's all just about keeping the Leader in power regardless, then the whole project is worthless. But I am writing for Leaders who do have a genuine desire to make change they believe in. And for these Leaders, from time to time—not too often and not on too major an issue— the business of politics demands concession to those you can rely on when the assassin moves from the street corner towards you, or the gangs turn on you, or the harmless passer-by mutates, or you become the target of an ambitious intriguer.

And there is another reason for creating and keeping a constituency: it will protect your legacy.

CHAPTER THIRTY-NINE

Protect Your Legacy

Protect your legacy, because, if you don't, no one else will.

It's easier said than done, however.

After a time in power, you forget what your previous life was like. You have become used to the rank, the trappings, the infrastructure like scaffolding beneath you keeping you aloft, and in the pulpit, or what Teddy Roosevelt called the "bully pulpit" (in those days the word "bully" meant more often wonderful, as in the old-fashioned English phrase "bully for you"). By pulpit, Roosevelt—that most remarkable of political Leaders and a study well worth the trouble all in himself—meant the power of the platform that being Leader of a country gives you. You can choose to be the first to speak—and you can usually have the last word too.

What you say matters. When you pronounce, people listen. With a minimum of skill, you can set the agenda because you're the Leader. Others can try, but you carry more weight. People can attack what you do, but they're reacting to your action. The microphone is always there in front of you. When you use it, no one else can match the volume.

That means you can also counter the naysayers. When opponents are rubbishing your achievements, you can defend your record loudly. When they're questioning your motives, you can answer their questions with authority. They can scream and bawl, hurl insults, make hurtful barbs against your record and your person, make accusations. But they can't silence you, or deprive you of that microphone and its power. They can besiege the pulpit and throw ordure at it, but you're still the one giving the sermon.

Once you step down, once you're out of the pulpit and another has taken your place in it, your whole world changes.

Gone is the power to command the microphone. Gone is the ability to speak louder and carry your voice further. Gone are the trappings, along with the rank. Gone is that infrastructure buoying you up.

Worse than being silenced, you can now be ignored.

And it's not just that. The person who comes after you will not necessarily see it as being in their interest to be supportive of or even fair to what you have done when in office. On the contrary, if from another tribe or party, it is entirely in their interest to be disobliging, to proclaim their inheritance as woeful, to present the challenges left in your wake as massively difficult. That way they can construct a narrative that allows them to excuse their own failings or inability to meet the expectations they have aroused to win power.

And even if your successor comes from your own party, they reasonably enough want to show that they're making a new start, adopting fresh thinking, shifting direction. Otherwise, they fear, people might wonder why them and not more of you?

As in other areas, you can profit more from my mistakes than by my achievements.

When I left office, I had big ambitions that did not include retirement. I wanted to do something different. I wanted to build something. And building takes work and focus. Seventeen years on, after a few false starts and rough patches, I feel I am, finally, in the place I wanted to be.

I chair an institute that is growing and that has a global reach, with teams of people all over the world helping governments make change. Which is good, but . . .

Because I had a new life with a new purpose, I thought I could leave the old life to take care of itself. Big mistake.

Inevitably, there were too many people with an interest in dissing my record. The Labour Party turned its back on New Labour because it wanted to show that a more traditional Labour Party was a better and more principled vehicle for progressive politics. The Conservative Party, which had suffered the shock for the first time since Labour's formation of three successive full terms of Labour in office, not unnaturally wanted to join in any discreditation to make sure Labour did not return to a winning formula. And to be fair, that part of the Conservative Party which was more centrist was itself coming under increasing attack from its own right wing.

I allowed a perfectly genuine and understandable disagreement and anger about Iraq and the post-9/11 support of America (which I do not dispute for a moment must be a major part of the assessment of my time in office) to eclipse almost completely the achievements—whether in improved services, cuts in poverty, economic growth, reduced crime, social and liberal advance, peace in Ireland, a minimum wage or our leadership in development.

Today things are a little different. When I left office, others were able and for sure willing to define my legacy in wholly negative terms. Now, with a changed Labour Party wanting power and understanding finally that the route to getting it is not dissimilar to the route I followed, at last there are defenders again. The fact remains, though, that I was unprepared; and I should have been prepared.

I have watched this happen repeatedly with other Leaders after they have relinquished power. Often for the noble and worthy reason of not wanting to get in the way of their successors, they go mute. And in general, that may well be right, as I say in the next chapter. But where your own record is being attacked, you should drag yourself out of silence and engage. At least periodically.

I always say I will take responsibility for the decisions I took in office, but not for those taken after that. An important elaboration on this is not to take responsibility for issues which may have started with your decisions but were then governed by the decisions of your successors. You take responsibility for your time when you were Leader. You don't take responsibility for what follows it.

Of course, it is much easier to protect your legacy when you have created a constituency that continues to be aligned with it, after you have left office. Then you have defenders.

However, all this gives you only a fighting chance—and I won't hide the difficulty of achieving this objective. Sometimes the best you can do is adopt the Zen spirit and hope!

Henry Kissinger once told me that he tried to comfort President Nixon, as he was leaving the White House following the Watergate scandal, by saying: "History will be kinder to you." Nixon replied: "It all depends on who writes the history, Henry."

Now that is not entirely the case: history does write itself to a degree, and, despite what some may think or believe, facts are still facts. But the colour, the interpretation, the framing of motive and impact, these are judgements, and the judges need at least to hear both sides.

So, you have to create the advocacy and the advocates. You must devote some of your time to answering the criticism and making your case.

You may have departed from power, but you haven't departed from memory. You need to work on rendering some of that memory as positive.

CHAPTER FORTY

Leaving with Grace

There is no perfect time to leave. No perfect time to be at the pinnacle and then off it. No perfect time to be "THE ONE" and then "the one before THE ONE."

Dictators can die in office. Democratically elected Leaders can leave because they have found something better to do. I can't, however, think of a case when that has occurred.

So, it's rarely a consented-to departure, not even when on the surface it appears to be.

In dictatorships, the motive for resisting departure is often fear. Most dictatorships involve a tight-knit group of people around the Leader. Generally, that tight-knit group have profited personally from their closeness to the source of their authority. Often, the Leader has participated in their schemes to accumulate riches or power. Their fear, therefore, is that a new Leader will take on the old, will see advantage in exposing the "wrongdoing" of the previous regime, and has their own entourage who expect to start their own self-aggrandising. That places both the old inner circle and the old Leader at risk. And in a dictatorship the leadership's response to risk can be more deadly than embarrassed.

In a democracy you may be term-limited. So, departure

from office at some point is inevitable. But that doesn't mean you're reconciled to it. Or you lose an election and never get that second mandate. Then you feel you have striven in vain. Or you're sacked, toppled, pushed, panicked or punished until the life force drains away and you crave release. Even then you don't really want to leave. Not really. Not deep down.

No one likes to go before the job is done, and as I said earlier, the job is never done. There is always a little bit of you and sometimes quite a lot of you that dwells on "unfinished business."

The fact remains, though, that at some point, sooner or later, go you must. You won't live forever and you won't lead forever.

So, how do you do it the right way? Is there a right way?

I believe it's possible to describe certain elements that may constitute a "right way."

First of all, recognise that you may be obliged to leave power when you sincerely believe you shouldn't. Reconcile yourself to it. Clinging on is not a good look, nor a good attribute. Be honest with yourself about it. Are you trying to stay because you think the country will be imperilled if you leave? Or is it an inner fear that the loss of power will mean a loss of face, even a loss of your faith in yourself; that when the thing which has come to define you passes, so will that self-definition?

Relinquishing power is never easy, especially if you feel your work is not finished, if the drive to govern for a reason is still present, if the fire in your own heart still burns. I mentioned earlier that it is an accompanying irony of

governing that—usually, though of course not universally—
the longer you govern, the better at it you become; and yet
your popularity is often in inverse proportion to your
capability.

So, you start at your most popular and least capable and
end at your least popular but most capable. I was, in truth,
a much better prime minister in my last five years in office
than in my first, at least in domestic policy, and by the time
I came to the ten-year mark, I had a real handle on how to
make change and the type of change that would be most
effective. But I knew my time was up; or, at least, up unless
I was prepared to engage in a full-frontal fight for survival
that could have harmed party and country.

Then there is the question of who succeeds you.

"Succession planning" in business has a whole industry
devoted to it. It is vital to the survival of the company. I can
think of good and bad examples.

When we come to politics, succession planning is every
bit as important and often more so, given we're talking
about the future of countries and not companies.

But the context for the planning is much, much more
complicated. And frankly, I can't think of many good
examples.

Most Leaders want to choose or, at least, play a part in
choosing their successor.

Their reasons can, of course, be bad or selfish. A Leader
might, for example, want to control the process because it
gives them a feeling of comfort—they're out but they still
count. Then it's just an extension of ego.

But their motives can also be honourable ones. The

country may be in a fragile state; it may be a democracy but a young one, prone to disorder. The opposition may genuinely be destructive of the best interests of the nation. Or, in a more developed country, it may be that there is a project of change and, as we have seen, changing a country often takes the time of more than one Leader.

Good Leaders have a project of advancement for their country. Those who stay after they have become unable to drive the project forward, or the project itself is no longer relevant, just occupy a space better occupied by others. But it's not wrong to try to make sure that there is some continuity, particularly where it is clear the direction in which the Leader took the country is reaping benefit for the people economically or politically.

Continuity in policy—where the policy is soundly based, of course—is an essential prerequisite for a successful country. It provides stability, gives time for a long-term reform to work; it helps set a direction. In democratic systems, this can be hard to achieve, since the natural disposition of an opposition is to oppose.

In a "not democratic" system, continuity of policy is easier to achieve while the regime is in office. But at some point, the regime changes and the same problem arises. So, the Leader should still take care to plan.

Succession, then, matters. Pay attention to it, even if you find that, when the moment comes, the power to affect it disintegrates. After all, politics is unpredictable. There is a multiplicity of different and occasionally warring interests; there are unexpected events which change the context of governing. All these conspire to make the circumstances and moment of departure hard to pinpoint and succession planning that much more difficult.

So, in leaving, try to make sure the future is in safe hands. But be realistic about who will take over. You are likely to lose the argument as often as you win it.

There is also something else which applies universally to succession planning for leadership: you can never really tell whether someone is up to the job until they have it. You can seek to assess their ability, and you would think if the newcomer has been near the top for a long time, you would be able to assess it with a high degree of accuracy. You would be wrong. You might think that your colleagues could judge who would be the best person to succeed. But they can as easily misjudge.

Finally, if you do manage to leave with a certain amount of grace, preserve it in the political afterlife.

That doesn't mean you become a hermit. Being a graceful former Leader is often confused with being a silent one. If an ex-Leader sees his or her country making what they believe is a serious error, or if they believe, as I did until recently, that their party is going in the wrong direction, they have, if not a duty, then at least a justification for speaking out.

But that is a different thing from deliberately undermining your successor because you hanker after a return; or becoming engaged in intrigue. In other words, if the issue is one of "big politics," fair enough. If it's small politics, your behaviour is ungracious and—by the way—usually futile.

I learnt a lesson early in adulthood about jealousy in love. Be friends with your ex. Preserve the friendship even if the close relationship has ended. Curb your inclination to bitterness, and conquer the chafing of your ego, even if, and maybe especially if, you've been dumped. You will feel better about yourself if you do so; and your ex may, in time, come to view you in a more positive light. Of course, they might not. But that's life.

If you can leave with grace, then do so. However you feel at the time of departure, you will feel better later.

Postscript

I am regularly asked: did you enjoy being prime minister? Truthfully, "joy" was never the word that came to mind in that context. Some Leaders I know will answer yes and some will even mean it. But, frankly, for me at least, there was too much stress, too great an awareness of responsibility, too heavy a sense of the weight of it all, to say "joy" when summarising how I felt. Fulfilled—yes. Engrossed and energised—certainly. But joy is what I feel on the birth of a child or grandchild, at a wedding or a celebration of someone else's achievement. In politics I felt it momentarily twice— when we concluded the Good Friday Agreement for peace in Northern Ireland, and when we won the bid to host the 2012 Olympics. But day to day I wasn't prancing around Downing Street joyfully.

However, it really is a privilege to lead a nation. And it is important to feel that. To understand that the Leader is in a privileged position. For one thing it makes the criticism bearable! But most of all, it conveys the notion that the Leader is there to serve. That's the deal: you're the boss, king or queen of the castle, numero uno; but the purpose of it all has to be grounded in the humility of service.

So, in a sense, your own feelings should be, need to be, relegated. Its "their"—i.e., the people's—feelings that matter.

And there is one thing—in addition to all the obvious things like they think you know what you're doing—which is worth a special mention. A country needs its spirits kept high.

A Leader needs to generate optimism.

No one wants to get on a plane with a depressed pilot. You want the person in charge of the plane to look like they have something to live for. They need to exude confidence, not anxiety.

People always remember the "blood, sweat and tears" part of the famous Churchill speech. And it's true he was explaining what a huge challenge we were facing. But it was all in the context of: we're going to win. At the end will be victory. The odds are mighty against us, but we will overcome.

Government is, of course, a serious business—or, at least, it should be. And because Leaders are engaged in it, dealing with issues of huge material importance to people, they can forget that for the most part, people don't really want to think a lot about politics or government. Political activists—who do think a lot about politics and government—often fail to understand this, or, if they understand it, are some-what disapproving of the public's general uninterest in their chosen obsession.

At the same time, never underestimate the people's desire for enjoyment, for pleasure, for entertainment. People "just wanna have fun" in the words of the song. OK, I am exag-gerating to make a point. But the point is an important one, which is that the seriousness of the business of governing, the difficult decisions which need to be made, the necessity of explaining the gravity of it all, must take account of the reality of human nature.

There is a wonderful description in Margaret MacMillan's book *Peacemakers*—about the negotiations held in Paris in 1919 to settle the issues arising out of the First World War—of how, despite the world- and nation-changing debates that were taking place, and the vastness of the matters at stake—the people who descended on Paris and the Parisians themselves still found ample time for fun. Theatres reopened, races recommenced at St. Cloud, new and daring dances and musicals were performed, and people, released from the horrors of war, had affairs and made love with all the passion and indulgence of which human beings are capable. Old inhibitions were loosened. Elinor Glyn, a famous romantic novelist of the time, wrote—rather disapprovingly it has to be said—of how: "Vice is rampant in Paris . . . Lesbians dine openly in groups of six sometimes, at Larue's. Men are the same." Even the Leaders—President Wilson, Lloyd George and Clemenceau—were prevailed upon to go out and relax.

So, when approaching the unavoidably sobering and occasionally dark business of government, leave a little space for some light and laughter.

This book has been about leadership in government. But the very idea of leadership assumes someone is following. And for people to follow, they need to believe the Leader is leading somewhere worth being led to. That their lives will be better, their nation better, the future better.

Indeed, the fact that it is a privilege to be the Leader should lend itself to optimism. You're in the position you have striven for. All things are possible within reason. Whether the nation advances is in your hands.

Of course, the test is ultimately if, together, Leader and people succeed. But you have an enlarged prospect of success if you start with a spirit which uplifts. Which is grounded in the humility that should accompany the privilege of leading and which ideally the Leader should naturally possess. Because, if it's not there by nature, it will be taught by experience.

Acknowledgements

This book is about leadership: how Leaders translate great ideas into delivery. I confess, though, that in my case it has taken quite a while to go from what I hope was a good idea to a delivered book. It's been a labor of love and one I would not have been able to complete without the help of the extraordinary team around me—in particular Daniel Sleat, who helped me with the research for this book. I would also like to thank everyone who works at my institute—which now operates in almost forty countries around the world and employs nearly 1,000 staff. They are an exceptional group of talented people dedicated to serving political leaders and governments.

At Penguin Random House, I would like to thank my publisher, Nigel Wilcockson. For reasons you won't need me to elaborate upon, he has come to be known in the office as "long-suffering Nigel." I am deeply grateful to him. Gail Rebuck, chair of Penguin Random House UK, also gave incredibly valuable advice on how to improve the text.

The lessons I draw in the book are from my experience both in office and since leaving Number Ten. Above, I thank the excellent staff at TBI who work supporting leaders around the world on strategy, policy, and delivery. Here, I want to thank the incredible ministers and dedicated people I had with me in government. It is thanks to them that there are the incredible achievements from our time in office to refer to.

ACKNOWLEDGEMENTS

Finally, a special thanks to all the leaders around the world I have been lucky enough to work with since leaving office. It has been, and remains, a privilege to engage with so many inspiring people on the front line of politics, working tirelessly to deliver improvements in the lives of their citizens.

Index